SOCIOLOGY OF DEVELOPMENT

SOCIOLOGY OF DEVELOPMENT

Sheobahal Singh

RAWAT PUBLICATIONS
Jaipur • New Delhi • Bangalore • Guwahati • Kolkata

ISBN 978-81-316-0360-4 (HB)

Reprinted, 2024

Published by
Prem Rawat for **Rawat Publications**
Satyam Apts, Sector 3, Jawahar Nagar, Jaipur 302 004 (India)
Phone: 0141 265 1748 / 265 7006
E-mail: info@rawatbooks.com
Website: www.rawatbooks.com

New Delhi Office
4858/24, Ansari Road, Daryaganj, New Delhi 110 002
Phone: 011 2326 3290

Also at *Bangalore*, *Guwahati* and *Kolkata*

Typeset by Rawat Computers, Jaipur

Printed and bound in India

Contents

Preface

Sociology of Development is one of the most popular courses in the colleges and universities in India. But, unfortunately, there has been a complete lack of study material on this. Having realized this as a university teacher for about four decades, this book is an attempt to provide students of both undergraduate and postgraduate levels with a comprehensive overview of the sociology of development.

Writing a textbook on a subject like development is really a challenging task. It is so because of the fact that the subject matter is quite complex and the changes in economy and society taking place in the world have been frequent, rapid and radical in the last two decades in the form of liberalization, privatization and globalization. Such conditions keep on generating new data and unfolding new laws and paradigms of development necessitating a fresh look at the problem and redefining development. Apart from the incessant changes taking place in social and economic conditions, we also witness uneven and inequitable pace and nature of development in different regions. Such variations are caused by varying soils, terrains, infrastructures, levels of education, urbanization and industrialization and above all differential impacts of governmental policies and political interventions.

The subject matter of sociology of development is indeed complex and onerous due to the interface between society and economy. Both condition each other and changes in one correspond to the changes in the other. The modern industrial economy could not have emerged if the culture would have not undergone radical changes, and the structural changes that we observe in family, community, social stratification and gender in our society today would not have become a reality, if radical changes would not have taken place in the economy and technology too.

Development not only implies economic development but also social development and political development. These three broad spheres of development are closely interlinked and determine the nature and extent of one another. Ever since the period of industrial development and Renaissance, so much has undergone transformation in the field of economy, society and polity that the scope of sociology of development has become terribly wide. The economy has changed from agrarian to industrial, subsistence to market, consumption to saving and investment. Social relations are no longer as authoritarian, emotional and familial as they were in the traditional society. They are now more or less democratic, rationalistic and individualistic. The polity also has undergone drastic change. The political system has switched from autocracy to democracy. Social exclusion has lessened and more and more participation of the weaker sections in the political processes of the country has now been confirmed. The downtrodden of the past have now become a formidable political force.

During the last two decades, the world, particularly its less developed parts, has experienced dazzling social, cultural and economic changes. Revolutionary advancement of the technology of mass communication, such as television, telephony, computer and internet, has accelerated the process of globalization.

This book is spread over ten chapters. The first chapter introduces to the reader the scope of sociology of development. The second, third and fourth chapters respectively deal with conceptual explanation and the theoretical interpretation of development and underdevelopment and identify the paths and agencies of development.

Indian students are going to benefit more from this book mainly because of the fact that the subject matter taken up in this volume and the examples given in support of the arguments have contextual connection with the conditions of India and other less developed nations. However, the conceptual and theoretical interpretations have wider relevance. Apart from discussing the developmental problems and issues as they exist, I have tried to present debates about the assumed bright as well as dark sides of technological and capitalistic development, as have been experienced in the present society.

I owe a great deal to Prof. Yogendra Singh, an eminent sociologist of India from whom I learnt sociology. This book is an outcome of the motivation I derived from my long association with Prof. K.L. Sharma. He has always been a source of inspiration to me.

I shall be happy if readers frankly communicate to me their objections to any part of this book for which I am solely responsible.

— **Sheobahal Singh**

1 Sociology of Development

There are several aspects of human life: social, economic, political, religious, familial, educational etc. All these aspects influence one another. Each of these aspects is studied by a separate discipline of social science. Economics and political science, for example, study economic and political aspects of life, respectively. Sociology likewise has several branches to study different aspects of social life. Thus, sociology of religion, sociology of education, sociology of medicine, sociology of entrepreneurship, sociology of law, sociology of crime and sociology of environment are such branches of sociology. Economic aspect of human life is perhaps the most vital one. Economic sociology, therefore, with its different branches like sociology of work, sociology of leisure, sociology of profession and sociology of development, holds a very significant position.

Sociology of development is a new branch of study. It originated with the post-Second World War and postcolonial experiences of development in the newly emerged nations. The need for sociological analysis of development emanated from the realization of an interface of economy and society. There is close linkage between socio-cultural environment and economic activities. Both condition each other. N.J. Smelser's book *Sociology of Economic Life* highlights relevant issues involved in the linkages between economy and society. People's attitudes towards economic activities and their philosophy of economic life are determined by the norms and values of the society they are brought up in. Karl Marx's thesis is that ideology, philosophy, norms, values and polity are determined by the economic structure. People's economic conditions determine their philosophy of social life and attitudes towards ethics, morality philanthropy, individual's dignity, humanity, law etc. Not only values but even day-to-day life activities are determined by economic conditions. The modern economic life with new kinds of jobs and professions on one hand, and women's active participation in gainful economic activities on the other, have posed new challenges to the traditional family system in India bringing about new household patterns. Traditional relationships between parents and children have changed. The size of family has reduced. The Indian family is no longer authoritarian. It has, instead, become democratic. Children and women are, in most cases, consulted on common issues. The nature of work has changed the living pattern in the family.

Max Weber's most popular thesis *Protestant Ethic and the Spirit of Capitalism* is perhaps the first and most convincing interpretation on the positive role of cultural norms in determination of the nature of economic milieu, as his study proved that Protestantism helped in bringing about modern capitalism in Western Europe.

Addressing the problems of development from the point of view of sociology may be called sociology of development. Development is a composite concept with multiple meanings. Economic development, social development, childhood development, political development, human development and sustainable development are various dimensions of development and all have sociological bearings. All these dimensions of development are, in one way or the other, interpretable in terms of their linkages with socio-cultural conditions. Economic development, for example, is not possible only when there is sufficient availability of economic factors like capital, labour, infrastructure, technological development, market, transportation and communication etc. These economic factors too need socio-cultural prerequisites which play a decisive role in making these factors effective.

Defining Sociology of Development

There are several branches of sociology, such as sociology of law, sociology of crime, sociology of environment, sociology of health and medicine, rural sociology, urban sociology, industrial sociology and political sociology. Sociology of development is likewise a branch of sociology. It studies the interface of socio-cultural circumstances and the processes of development. This discipline presumes that every aspect of development largely depends on sociological conditions of society for its realization. For example:

- Economic development depends on entrepreneurship development and entrepreneurship is a socio-psychological phenomenon.
- Market and consumption patterns are socially determined.
- Several sociological conditions define development. Gender equity, women's education and their participation in economically gainful activities, increase of lifespan, increase of literacy, advancement of democracy, reduction of infant mortality, reduction of maternal deaths, reduction of death rate and birth rate are the sociological phenomena which in combination determine the extent of development.
- Sociology of development deals not only with industrialization and economic growth in a country but also enquires into the relationships emerging as a consequence of economic development. Theories of underdevelopment and dependency are thus hot subjects of sociology of

development today as the gap between the rich and poor countries is increasing and the latter are underdeveloped and dependent on developed countries which exploit them.

- Traditional societies do not offer the values which help development. Conformism, intransigence, dogmatism and irrationalism do not facilitate development. Modernization is a basic prerequisite for promotion of development. That is why, most characteristics of modernization and development are common.
- Variations among different countries and different regions of a country exist not only because of differential infrastructural conditions but largely due to differential socio-cultural potentials among them.

The scope of sociology of development would most appropriately be understood by making a distinction between the classical economics and the development economics that emerged around the earlier years of the second half of the last century. The classical or traditional economics was purely a study of political economy which dealt with the relationship between politics and economics and analyzed the economic laws of monopoly and dominance. Management of resources, markets and their best appropriation and sustaining growth have been the prime substance of study.

The development economics has much wider scope of study. According to M.P. Todaro, the development economics, in addition to being concerned with the efficient allocation of existing scarce productive resources and with their sustained growth over time, must also deal with the economic, social and institutional mechanisms, both public and private, necessary for bringing about rapid (at least by historical standards) and large-scale improvements in level of living for the poverty-stricken, malnourished, illiterate people of Africa, Asia and Latin America. The development economics thus concerns much with structural and institutional transformations and human development. Sociology of development is quite close to development economics with the only difference that the former locates sociological laws and spheres that contribute to development and what social and cultural consequences are entailed from development whereas the latter is concerned with the task of tracing the cultural and institutional conditions which determine development in a society.

Todaro is convinced that economics is a social science. It is concerned with human beings and the social systems by which they organize their activities to satisfy their basic material (food, shelter, clothes) and non-material needs (education, knowledge, spiritual fulfilment). The economics can claim neither scientific laws nor universal truths. Economic investigations and analyses, therefore, cannot simply be lifted out of their institutional, social and political context, especially when one must deal with the human dilemmas of hunger, poverty and ill-health, which plague greater portion of the world's population. Todaro pleads for the necessity of recognizing ethical or normative value premises about what is or is not the desirable central feature of the economic discipline in general and of development economics in particular. The concepts or goals, such as economic and social equality, elimination of poverty, universal education, rising standards of living, national independence, modernization of institutions, political and economic participation, grassroots democracy, self-reliance and personal fulfilment all derive from subjective value judgements about what is good and desirable and what is not.

Sociology of development is thus a social science discipline which studies economic development from the point of view of social development. It attempts to explore the linkages between social, cultural, political and institutional spheres, and the levels of economic development in a society. The discipline tries to understand how far the social, cultural, political and institutional factors are facilitative or inhibitive to development. The ultimate aim of the subject is to trace the non-economic factors of economic development.

Sociology of development is not primarily concerned with the analysis of economic development at micro and macro levels in terms of the magnitude of economic development linked with economic variables. It takes into account the economic performance only to assess the role of social and cultural factors in this and suggests socio-cultural requirements of development. Sociology of development is, instead, primarily concerned with the nature of relationships emerging among nations and different regions in a nation. The relationships, which have so far been observed by the economists and sociologists, are essentially of dependency as the nature of development is capitalist, of which underdevelopment and dependency are the natural corollary. The world system theory is an intellectual by-product of this kind of development.

Scope of Sociology of Development

We have learnt in the preceding section that development is a wide concept that encompasses all the three spheres of development, viz., economic, social and political, in its ambit. Development is thus an inclusive concept. While social and cultural factors determine the nature and extent of economic development, the political factors also bring about changes in the social and cultural spheres of the society. The linkages between economic and non-economic aspects of a society thus form the scope of study of sociology of development. Following are the areas that the sociology of development suggests to be explored:

Structure and Development

Social structure has been studied extensively by scholars to establish its positive or negative role. It has been observed, for example, that the traditional social structure, which had been authoritarian in nature and in which the status rights and duties of an individual were ascribed and not achieved, did not facilitate the process of development. The micro-structures, such as joint family and caste system, and the macro-structures, such as modern elite and bureaucracy, need to be studied with an objective to find out their positive and negative role in development. Indian caste system and joint family system have been only contested concepts as far as their role in economic development is concerned. K. Sujata, Timberg, Berna, Sheobahal Singh Chaudhary etc. may be consulted to discover the linkages between social structure (family, caste) and business in India.

Culture and Development

It is not only social structure but also the culture, which determines the nature and magnitude of development in a society, forms part of scope of sociology of development. Religious compatibility and imperativeness of cultural reform have proved to be culturally conducive factors for development and, therefore, are important to be introduced into the curriculum of sociology of development. Similarly, humanistic and liberal philosophical orientations of people towards social, religious and economic life are the issues, which need to be addressed in this discipline. Max Weber, Kapp, Papaneck and Momin have put forth their views on these lines.

Entrepreneurship and Development

As stated earlier, development refers to social and cultural development along with successive economic growth. Industrialization and economic growth do not result only from a precondition of sufficient infrastructure, comprising capital, technology and labour, but most importantly, from adequate supply of able entrepreneurs. An entrepreneur is not a capitalist nor is he/she a simple trader. Entrepreneur is a business leader, who takes initiative to instal a business enterprise even by way of innovation. Entrepreneur is an extraordinary person with a typical personality, who emerges from a specific social and cultural milieu and is, therefore, a subject of study for both sociologists and psychologists. Entrepreneurship is thus an important part of the scope of sociology of development.

Polity and Development

As already stated, political factors play a very significant role in development. No factor of development, howsoever strong it is, will remain ineffective to yield results unless it is supported by governmental policies and programmes. Industrial policies of governments have great bearing upon entrepreneurial development and industrial expansion. Incentive, support and protection are important roles a government has to perform in order to ensure economic development in the country. Unequal industrial development among different states in our country is due to inter alia variations in their industrial policies. Political factors need to be taken into consideration by sociologists while analyzing development of a country.

Human Development Index

Life expectancy, literacy, infant mortality, death rate and birth rate have been included by UNO in the Human Development Index (HDI). A country, according to HDI, must record successively growing rate of life expectancy and literacy and declining rate of infant mortality, death and birth in order to be labelled as a developing country. The level of development of different countries is rated on the scale of HDI. The lower the index of a country, the lesser developed it is. Thus, HDI forms an important part of the scope of sociology of development.

Sustainability of Development

From around the mid-eighties of the last century, people became conscious of the negative consequences of the nature of development pursued earlier. Two main problems of development noticed were environmental pollution and depletion of natural resources. These two dangerous offshoots of the development, based on the use of technology and cruel exploitation of natural resources, posed serious threat to living creatures. The efforts since then started to mobilize people to move on a path of development which may sustain instead of threatening lives on the earth. To explore viable alternatives to the existing developmental planning and methods is now a serious challenge before scholars of development.

Displacement and Rehabilitation of People

Displacement of people is an oft-happening corollary of the development projects executed by governments. This is a great social problem as well. Displaced families need to be adequately rehabilitated, for which the states have to frame well-thoughtout policies, which may ensure minimum decent living and appropriate compensation. India still is a major agricultural and rural economy and most of people in its countryside are either small and marginal peasants and farmers or a landless folk. The development projects, most of which have the countryside under their coverage, mostly affect the marginal and weaker sections of the area. The big landowners are not much affected in terms of their standard of living, instead, they gain quite often much more from the developmental projects carried out than they lose from them. Social, ethical and legal issues are involved in the after-effects of development projects. If corruption is so rampant that it seems to replace the supreme value of honesty in a society, the condition has got to be nastiest. We have been experiencing this for the last five decades with reference to land reforms and community development programmes. The rehabilitation policies of the Government of India need to be analyzed sociologically in terms of the level of satisfaction of those who are displaced and in lieu compensated across different sections of society.

Modernization of Traditions

Huntington has pointed out that modernity and development have many symptoms in common. A society may not develop unless and until its traditions undergo a process of modernization. The study of change in Indian society is still problematic because of the fact that Indian traditions are so deep in history that they have not been completely replaced with modernity. The trajectory of modernization in India has put the Indians, particularly the middle class on crossroads, where they are guided to be partly modern and partly traditional. This ambivalence has caused a constrained development in the country. Yogendra Singh and Milton Singer have observed the trajectory of modernity in the world of Indian traditions. The study of sociology of development is, in a way, the study of modernization in a society.

Gender and Development

How can a society boast to be developed or developing if women are discriminated and denied status parallel to men in a society. The traditional family structure of civilized societies, almost world over, has been patriarchal and bigoted to women. Almost half of the population being denied participation in general social and political spheres would negate any symptom of social development, but more alarming is the denial of their participation in gainful economic activities. This has been accruing great economic loss to the society. Women's work cannot be underrated. But, unfortunately, according to a UN report, about three-fourths of unmonetized labour in the world is done by women. In most of the societies, which are not fully developed, women are denied opportunities and privileges of participation on an equal plane with men not only in political and economic spheres but also in day-to-day activities with regard to health and hygiene. It is, therefore, recommended that one of the most significant areas in the foci of sociology of development shall be gender discrimination.

2 Development

Concept and Paradigms

Change is the law of nature. Society, polity, economy, geography and culture – all undergo a ceaseless process of change. All structural categories like caste, family and market and cultural categories like customs, traditions, values, ideologies, art and artifacts come under this process. Development, progress and evolution are different concepts to denote different modes of change. Some changes are self-propelled and perfunctory and others intended, planned and pursued. Changes in the structure and culture of society are largely of evolutionary nature. However, the traditional normative patterns are not completely displaced. Factors of change in society are both endogenous as well as exogenous. The changes other than the planned and intended ones are essentially value-free and their direction and nature are self-determined. Changes in the structural domains like caste, family, polity and bureaucracy and the changes in cultural domains like style of life, values and attitudes towards rituals and religious practices, nation and nationality, traditions and customs are examples of socio-cultural changes in society.

Development, on the other hand, is a planned change in the material conditions and related socio-cultural milieu.

The concept of development, like modernization, appeared in academic writings only after the second quarter of the 20th century when scholars became attentive to the problems of development in Asian, African and Latin American countries which became independent one after the other and set out on the path of planned growth of their economies. The scholars, keeping in mind the conditions of these so-called Third World countries, arrived at the conclusion that the problems of development in the developing countries were more non-economic than economic. It was also realized that these colonial countries were not moving fast on the path of development because of their inhibitive social and cultural conditions. It was conceived that the cause of the sluggish pace of their development was not necessarily the dearth of capital, labour, technology and raw material but the tradition-bound social structure and culture. Max Weber and W. Kapp have held that the Hindu religion and caste system were responsible for the slow pace of development in India. However, this view may not be accepted without reservation. Since caste and occupation were traditionally linked with each other through religion, social and occupational mobility has been to a very limited extent. However, occupational mobility in Indian society has never been absolutely absent as opined by the Western writers. Keeping in view all these points, it may be safely said that certain structural and cultural conditions have definitely played a crucial role in the inhibited state of development in India.

Modernization and Development

Modernization and development, due to historical and contextual similarities, are so close to each other that these are often used interchangeably. Modernization refers to the change in attitude and orientation of people towards such a pattern of life, the outcome of working on those lines is called development. The early writings on modernization had two basic theoretical orientations: one, economic and technological development brings about change in culture and social structure as it happened in the West; and two, there has been the effect of innovation, technology and development of the West on the non-industrialized societies.

The theory of modernization sprouted from the functionalist sociology of Talcott Parsons. Parsons wrote how the relationships change when a society transits from non-industrial to industrial one. He draws a list of five specific dichotomous choices (pattern variables) which would determine role orientations. In the case of a non-industrial society transforming into an industrial one, the changes in relationship have been depicted even before Parsons in the evolutionary perspective in sociology. Emile Durkheim presented change in society from mechanical to organic solidarity and Ferdinand Tonnies distinguished gemeinschaft from gesellschaft in the same sense to express the shift.

S.C. Dube identifies three points which are common to both the concepts:

(i) Modernization is a process of change which distinguishes between three stages of society, viz., traditional, transitional and modern.
(ii) Development makes distinction between undeveloped, developing and developed societies.
(iii) The concept of modernization is evolutionary.

Historically, almost all the societies have moved, after Renaissance, on the path of modernization – a process of change in society, where people's actions are based on rationality, innovation and excessive use of technology. Samuel P. Huntington points out the following nine characteristics of modernization, which are also used as indices of development:

1. Modernization and development are radical processes of change in technology and culture. These may be identified

with the change from nomadic to agrarian age and the current change from agrarian to urban-industrial culture.

2. These are complex and multidimensional processes linked with cognitive, behavioural and institutional reform and structural reformations in society.
3. These are grand processes which originate at a place and then encompass other parts of the world with their ideology and technology.
4. These are long-term processes and develop in due course.
5. Both the concepts are systematic and change in one dimension entails change in others.
6. These processes involve several stages of change.
7. These are homogenizing processes under which variations between societies are reduced.
8. Both are irreversible processes, with occasional inconsistencies and commotions.
9. These are progressive, indispensable and desirable processes and contribute in the long run to physical and cultural prosperity of human beings.

It is important to note that the processes of development and modernization, except for a few aspects of them, have not been found to be uniform and ubiquitous in the world. Modernization is only partial and culture-specific. Talcott Parsons' views on universalization of culture under the canvas of modernization would not stand verified. Development has been unequal and dissimilar and has widened gap among individuals, groups, societies and nations in terms of their achievements. Alvin Toffler expresses his concern that only a small part of the world has been successful in the efforts of modernization and development.

How to Define Development?

Defining development is not an easy task. It is so primarily because of the fact that the concept of development is impregnated with social, cultural, political and economic dimensions intertwined with one another and also because of many paradigm changes this process has undergone so far. Its composite and multidimensional nature has made it really difficult for the scholars to formulate one all-encompassing definition of development. It can be explained only in terms of material and non-material changes viewed as betterment through history and in the contexts of different ramifications of such changes.

Changing Paradigms of Development

The concept of development is not very old. As stated at the outset, it came in currency only by the second half of the preceding century perhaps only when most of the present-day less developed countries emerged as independent nations after their long subjugation to the colonial rule and set out on the path of their own planned economic progress. Development, like modernization, is a concept, which was used to analyze the level of social, economic and political progress in colonial countries on the lines of progress attained by the West after the Renaissance and the Industrial Revolution. Social, political and economic changes that took place in Western Europe became the parameters of development and modernization to assess the level of progress made by the developing countries on this path. That is why, though Adam Smith's *Wealth of Nations* is treated as the first treatise on development economics, a systematic study of development began only in the middle of the 20th century when problems of developing countries attracted attention of economists and other social scientists. Development, therefore, emerged as a relative concept which presupposed a comparison of the less developed countries of Asia, Africa and Latin America with the developed countries of the West. There has been periodic paradigm shift in the concept of development ever since its inception in academic writings. This shift has been in correspondence with the changing experiences of development in the less developed countries and the ideological approach of looking at development and progress in society. Below we discuss various perspectives on development and the changes made over time.

Economic Growth Perspective

In the writings of early economists, the concept of development, as we define today, is missing. These writings have confined themselves to what we treat as economic growth and explained the concept only rationally and in economic terms. The progress could be measured in terms of per capita income, GNP, and the number of functioning industrial units. They looked at development from this angle, and referred essentially to the successive growth in material and manual forces of production like land, labour, capital and technology.

The theories of economic growth vary in their views but there are four common points in them which explain the laws of economic growth:

1. the accumulation of capital and improvement of technology,
2. population change,
3. the division of labour into specialized activities, and
4. entrepreneurship.

Adam Smith, writing in the beginning of 18th century, propounded the first systematic theory of economic growth. According to him, invention of better machines is responsible for increase in productivity and material welfare. The classical economics stressed upon development in terms of economic growth and believed that if annual growth is at the rate of 5 to 6 per cent, it should be treated as a developing economy. W.A. Lewis, one of the celebrated economists of classical era, has favoured per capita production to distribution.

For Karl Marx, the determining force in history is technology. Technology, according to him, would hasten polarization of classes and intense class struggle leading to the unity of workers against capitalists and seizing power from them.

Adam Smith and David Ricardo were of the view that an increase in population growth would reduce the rate of economic growth. But, later on, English economist John Maynard Keynes' theory rejected the thesis of Smith and Ricardo and stressed that an increase in population increases demand for goods, which stimulates investment and ultimately economic growth. The last two decades of economic achievements of China and India – the two most populous countries of the world – have also proved that population explosion is perhaps not necessarily a detrimental force in economic development.

Accumulation of capital and economic growth lead to division of labour and vice versa. Division of labour refers to specialization of production functions which increases skills among workers and skilled and specialized work leads to increase in productivity. Smith emphasizes the role of division of labour in the increase in production.

Entrepreneurship – a key factor in economic growth – was in fact not recognized in the early economics. However, Ricardo did regard the role of capitalist as visionary investor and organizer of rent of land, wages and production, which is paramount in economic growth. But, the capitalist is not necessarily an entrepreneur. Joseph Schumpeter, much later, gave a systematic definition of an entrepreneur and emphasized her/his role of an innovator as a key factor in economic development.

Human Development Perspective

The concept of human development has its origin in the writings of early economists like Adam Smith, David Ricardo, Robert Malthus, John Stuart Mill etc., but over time, excessive preoccupation with income growth obscured this objective of development. It is the United Nations Development Programme (UNDP), which revived the concept in its Human Development Report (HDR) of 1990 (UNDP, 1990). This could be done only by realizing the fact that economic growth may not be termed as realistic and down-to-earth development as the growth of wealth would not necessarily ensure that nobody would really be hungry. Human development broadly refers to improvement in the overall human well-being. This focuses on the human face of development and this perspective could emerge on realizing that there is no automatic relationship between the growth of GNP and improvement in the quality of life. Sri Lanka, Chile, Jamaica, Thailand and Tanzania, for example, have done far better on their human development ranking than on their income ranking, whereas Oman, Saudi Arabia, Algeria and Senegal have a much higher income ranking than their human development ranking (UNDP, 1990: 14–16). China, India and Pakistan have almost similar per capita GNP level but human development performance of China is much better than the other two countries.

It is not easy to measure the level of quality of life and people's relative deprivation in this context. However, the UNDP (1990) has introduced Human Development Index (HDI), which may be used to measure relative human development position. The indicators, which have been identified to measure the level of human development include (a) life expectancy, (b) literacy rate, (c) birth rate, (d) death rate, and (e) infant mortality rate. India's position is very sad as it ranks 126th out of 177 countries of the world.

In India, the death rate declined from 14.9 in 1971 to 8.9 in 1997, the infant mortality rate from 129 in 1971 to 80 in 1991 and further to 71 in 1997. The birth rate also declined from 36.9 in 1971 per thousand to 29.5 in 1991 and further to 27.2 in 1997. However, if we look at the inter-state variations, we find that there are wide variations. For example, the life expectancy in

Kerala is 72, which is much higher than that of Bihar, Madhya Pradesh, Orissa, Rajasthan and Uttar Pradesh. Kerala's performance is comparable with the other Asian countries like China, Malaysia, Indonesia, Thailand and Sri Lanka, which have made significant progress in human development over the years.

The reduction in death rate, birth rate and infant mortality rate in India is visibly significant though not so encouraging if compared with that of developed countries and some of the developing countries. The increase in health care and family welfare services in India has contributed significantly to the performance it has made in the human development sector.

However, there are wide inter-state variations in human development performance levels. For example, Kerala with life expectancy at 72 and literacy at 90 is far ahead of the states like Bihar, Madhya Pradesh, Orissa, Rajasthan and Uttar Pradesh, where the quality of life of people is terribly poor.

The economists concentrating on the problems of Asian, African and Latin American countries realized that the existing social, cultural and economic conditions of these countries required radical transformation in order to move on the road of development. Culture and economy in these countries had been primarily agrarian and poverty, illiteracy and traditional outlook were dominant features. The economists needed an apparatus to understand the problems and the levels of development in these countries. They tried to undertake this keeping in mind the history and culture of the then developed countries. Hence, a comparative approach.

However, the multidimensional process of development involves reorganization and reorientation of the entire system – economic, social and cultural. Michael P. Todaro wrote that development, along with economic development, involves radical changes in institutional, social and administrative structures as well as people's attitudes, customs and beliefs. Thus, development is not merely an improvement in material conditions and the standard of living of people of a society; it also includes and perhaps precludes improvement in human index in terms of life expectancy, infant mortality, adult literacy and social conditions of people. The decades of 60s and 70s of the 20th century were treated as the "development decades" by the United Nations which also resolved that if a country achieves the target of 6 per cent or more annual growth rate of GNP it should be designated as a developing economy. Thus, the UN defined development in terms of 6 per cent of GNP growth.

But, later on, it was felt that despite achieving the growth target set by the UN, the masses could not be freed from the trap of poverty and unemployment in most of these countries. This led to redefining the concept of economic development with more emphasis on the distribution part of economy and the gross income achieved by the state. Economic development during 70s was then redefined in terms of reduction or elimination of poverty, inequality and unemployment within the context of growing economy. This redefinition of development was made at the instance of Dudley Seers, who questioned the claim of development if poverty has not been arrested and if unemployment and inequality have increased.

Social Development Perspective

The concept of social development gained currency at the time when the Third World countries started to strive for economic development. The scholars and the agencies like UNO, working on the problems of development in the developing countries, realized that these countries due to prolonged colonial subjugation were left with sad social and economic conditions at the time of independence and were far away from modern values. This state of affairs subjected these countries to many constraints on the path to economic development. Therefore, what was required of these countries was to adopt policies and planning for the social development of their societies on priority basis.

The concept of social development, according to M.S.A. Rao, is inclusive of economic development but differs from it in the sense that it emphasizes the development of the society in its totality – including economic, political, social and cultural aspects. In this sense, social development planning is not concerned with planning exclusively for social services any more but it is also concerned with the planning for economic growth. There are many areas, apart from social or welfare services, wherein the social perspective has relevance, e.g., population policy, policy relating to urbanization, industrial location and environmental pollution, regional development, income growth, income distribution and land reform, policies governing administration and people's participation in planning and the implementation of plans.

Social development is a broad concept which refers to the development of society a whole. The processes of social development are both means and ends in themselves. A society gradually evolves into a modern society with a rational outlook and scientific temper. People are not sentimentally attached to traditional forms of social structure and values and are easily adaptive to change, oriented to welcome innovations and ready to move on a new path. They are not dogmatic, gullible and superstitious. Social structure is democratic and not authoritarian as the traditional societies used to be. The political system is secular and democratic. Citizens enjoy autonomy and freedom to choose a path for themselves within the constitutional confines.

Social development and economic development are mutually complementary processes. The progress in one necessarily conditions progress in the other. The term 'social' is not precise enough to be understood easily. There is distinction between social and psychological terms like attitudes, motivations, ideas and values but treating the term 'social' in opposition to the term 'economic' would include these psychological terms within the sphere of social. The concept 'social' consists of all non-economic factors. Social development is a pre-condition for economic development. According to J.A. Ponsoien, social is an autonomous field and, therefore, social development has to be defined in its own terms. The changes in the social field which are compatible and conducive to economic development may be defined as social development.

The spheres, which are indicative of the social realms, according to J.A. Ponsoien, are as follows:

1. The cultural and mental background from which individuals operate and which causes their willingness or unwillingness, their fitness or unfitness to take up various tasks in the economic development.
2. The institutions and social structures, types of groups and social organizations, through which the people are able to cope with these tasks for collective as well as for individual purposes or, in other words, which enable them to bring their mental background into use.
3. The regulations of a society which enable individuals to cope financially with the opportunities offered, this being done through redistribution of income or by special grants in case of need or unexpected drop in income.
4. The welfare services of a society by which individuals are assisted who, through lack of finance, knowledge or capacity, are unable to meet their own needs, so that these have to be covered with the help of others.

Sustainable Development Perspective

By the end of 70s of the last century, it was realized that the nature and extent of development, as was conceived and being pursued, would harm more than help the mankind. Cruel exploitation of the natural resources (the ultimate source of our life) reduced them to a lamentable level. The backwash effect of the blind race in achieving the kind of development as is done so far emerged in the form of ecological imbalance, environmental degradation and pollution of water and air. Also, there seemed to be a potential crisis of energy – the most necessary part of development. These alarming conditions forced scholars to contemplate about an approach to development which would minimize these threats. This led to the emergence of the concept of sustainable development. The approach of sustainable development refers to the method of development which may, on the one hand, bring about better standard of living and life chances and, on the other, the possibility of negative impact of the process of development may be minimal. This involved the widening of the concept of development to include a part of social development of awareness among people to be sensitive to the imperativeness of maintenance of ecology and conscious and careful management of development problems to avoid any danger to the living world.

There must be a limit to economic growth. This could be realized when environmental misbalance and ecological attrition appeared as an apparent necessary offshoot of this growth. The 'green movement' arose world over and people became concerned about environmental problems and started conserving and protecting the natural resources and animal species as a response to the report 'The Limits Growth' published in the early 1970s by the Club of Rome – a group formed by the industrialists, business advisers and civil servants of Italy. The report warned that the current rates of industrialization and development would be unsustainable due to pollution of air and water and depletion of the natural resources. Anthony Giddens, in his book *Sociology*, has discussed the criticism labelled against the views in the report of the Club of Rome. The main criticism was that the report considered only the physical limits of the growth and ignored the role of market forces, which work to keep balance between available resources, demand and supply, and the capacity of human being to respond to the environmental challenges of technological growth. The view that economic development should be limited was also criticized as pointless and it was argued that economic development should be promoted and less developed countries should not be barred from their own process of development.

The debate on the limits of growth and the promotion of growth with environmental consciousness led to the development of the idea of sustainable development. The term first appeared in the 1987 report 'Our Common Future' of the United Nations. Sustainable development was defined by the Brundtland Commission as meeting of "the needs of the present without compromising the ability of future generation to meet their own needs". Since the publication of the report, the concept of sustainable development gained currency the world over and attracted the attention of environmentalists, NGOs and governments. United Nations, in particular, has been attentive since then and organizing summits with agenda of sustainable development. Economic development without considering its impact on environment and adopting measures to protect it from ill-effects of development would be fatal for the human society. The concept of sustainable development aims at maximizing the net benefits of economic activities, subject to maintaining the stock of productive assets (physical, human and environmental) over time and providing a social safety net to meet the basic needs of the poor. Sustainable development attempts to accelerate development in an environmentally responsible manner keeping in mind the intergenerational equity requirements (Economic Survey of India, 1998).

Indicators of Social Development

Social development, as stated earlier, encompasses social, political and cultural domains of society. The following are the various indicative points in different domains, which help us analyze social development:

Social Aspects

1. The society is more modern and less traditional.
2. The society is more democratic and less authoritarian.

3. The social status is largely determined by achievements and not by birth as in the traditional caste-based society. Social discrimination, if at all exists, is determined by acquired attributes of individuals and not by where they are born.
4. The structure of family is no longer authoritarian and large in size as the traditional joint family used to be. It is small household, nuclear type and democratic in nature as the most urban families seem to be today. Size of kinship structure in traditional societies used to be large. With social development, it is circumscribed. It is being experienced that the family of procreation and kin people from wife's family of orientation are occupying dominant place in family relationship.
5. There is no religion-based hierarchical division of society.
6. The society is urbanized and the general way of life of people is urban. Rural-to-urban and urban-to-urban migrations are high in a developing society.
7. Social and occupational mobility in society is unrestricted and fast. For example, the traditional Indian caste system had relatively restricted social and occupational mobility. The modern Indian society is now least caste-bound in its social and connubial interactions and occupational choice. However, the Indian society is still largely endogamous.
8. Various governmental and non-governmental agencies are developed to carry out the responsibilities traditionally being carried out by the family. For example, crèche, old age homes, home delivery of commodities from the market and the like.
9. The rate of population growth is lower.
10. Rates of mortality, including maternal deaths and infant mortality, are also lower.
11. Literacy rates – both male and female – are high.
12. Health facilities are expanded and made available to all – from top to the bottom in the class structure.

Cultural Aspects

1. Attitude of people in developed societies is essentially individualistic, materialistic and profit-oriented. Maximization of achievements is the goal of people.
2. Primeval sentiments are no longer dominant in the social behaviour of individuals. Human behaviour is largely governed by existing situations. Casteism, racism, familialism, fundamentalism, dogmatism and so on are faded and phased out in the wake of social development. People become secular and humanist in their value-orientation.
3. Nationalism and pluralism develop along with social development.
4. The institutions and agencies of human rights grow.
5. The value orientation of a modern person in a developed society is more individual and family-centred and not community-centred. What is to be done or not to be done is determined only by how much satisfaction the individual derives from that action.
6. Customs and traditions become weak. The rate of change in the context of social intercourse, foodstuff, clothes and housing pattern is accelerated. Food habits undergo change to become more metropolitan and continental.
7. Religions and the believers exist but religious practices and rites seem to be on the wane.
8. People become more rational and less superstitious and dogmatic.

Political Aspects

Democracy is the most acceptable form of political system in the developed and developing societies. Except a few countries like Myanmar, Pakistan, Nepal and Bhutan, which do not fall in the category of sound democracies, most of the countries of the world have democracy of one form or other. The kind of social process, which started to evolve with the Renaissance, was named as modernization and development and the first and most radical form of social change that took place in the process was the disjunction of Church from polity and the establishment, in its place, of democracy.

Some characteristics of political development are:

1. Nation and nationhood develop.
2. Liberty to every citizen is ensured. People enjoy freedom of speech, choice of profession, practice of religion, etc.
3. The state is secular. It does not discriminate one citizen from the other on the basis of caste, creed, religion and region.
4. State seeks to guarantee equality among its citizens. Equality does not mean according equal status to everyone, because, an absolutely egalitarian society is perhaps only utopian. True meaning of equality is to ensure equal opportunity to all. Indian Constitution, for example, guarantees equal opportunity to every citizen to participate in the political, social, economic and cultural activities in the country.
5. Consciousness about the human rights and civil society develops with social development and maturity of democracy. The state and the non-governmental organizations (NGOs) become concerned about these matters and the welfare of citizens gains paramount attention.

Environmental Degradation

Environmental degradation is caused by mainly two kinds of pollution: air pollution and water pollution. Air and water are perhaps the two most important parts of environment, the availability of which in sufficient and uncontaminated form is a necessary condition for human life. Both air and water pollution and the unmanageable level of waste products, due to industrial development, urban explosion and rising consumption of food and fuel, are the major factors causing ecological imbalance.

Air Pollution

Air pollution is a serious problem being faced by people the world over today. Air pollution is caused by emission of gases from chimneys of manufacturing units, automobiles and the fuel used in homes for heating and cooking. According to a recent Human Development Report, more than 2.7 million people die of air pollution every year in the world, of which 90 per cent deaths occur in the developing world.

In less developed countries, air pollution is caused by the use of coal, cow dung and wood for heating and cooking purposes in homes emitting smoke and dangerous gas like carbon dioxide (CO_2). In rural areas, these are used unabatedly. Also, the old motor vehicles continue to ply on the road for long periods of time, which discharge more fumes than the new ones.

In urban areas and developed countries, air pollution is largely caused by industries and motor vehicles. Vehicles and industrial units are increasing fast even in the less developed countries to cause similar kind of pollution problem there. Vehicular pollution is becoming a serious threat because of the fact that people on roads are directly affected by the emission from the vehicles. School-going children in Indian cities are most vulnerable to air pollution as they are in the closest contact with toxic emissions on the roads. As a result, they are suffering from respiratory problems, insomnia etc.

Both population growth and economic development contribute to a large extent of emission of CO_2. It has been projected that during the period 1991–2025, the population growth alone will contribute 54 per cent of the CO_2 emissions and during the following 75 years – 2025-2100 – their contribution will decline by 13 per cent (Chaudhary, 1995). The considerable scale of decline in the population growth rate in India thus will bring about a substantial environmental improvement in the long run. The best environmental policy would, therefore, be the one which ensures a rapid decline in population growth in the country.

Water Pollution

Water is the most important natural resource for life. Human being needs water not only for drinking but also for cooking, washing, irrigation, fishing etc. People have been abusing and misusing water since long. Industrial wastes, garbage and other remains of used commodities have been getting dumped in rivers and oceans causing contamination of water. It is also contaminated of toxic chemicals discharged from factories, pesticides used in agriculture and so on. Due to the poor water supply system, contact of sewage with the warer supply line contaminates water used for drinking. Contaminated water has become a serious threat to human beings, fish and the animals. The poor and less developed countries are facing greater problem of water pollution as they have dilapidated water treatment and supply system and also lack in proper waste disposal system. They dispose waste products and garbage straight away in their rivers and lakes. About one-third population of the world does not have access to safe water. A very common water-borne disease is diarrhoea, which is caused by contaminated water. It is very common in poor countries and in the segment of poor people of less developed countries.

Developed countries are almost free from the problem of water pollution. Pollution of water in those countries is mainly due to the excessive use of pesticides to protect agricultural crops. Water pollution in these countries is not due to the lack of management of garbage as in the less developed countries for whom its disposal and treatment is normally unaffordable.

However, the developed countries are not confronted with the problem of water contamination as much as the poor ones because they have sufficient resources and efficient technology for treatment and recycling of sewage, garbage and domestic waste.

A team of researchers at Britain's Centre for Ecology and Hydrology and experts from World Water Council introduced a new index of water-rich and water-poor countries. Five different criteria were used to construct the index: resource, access, use, capacity and environment. This water index is not congruent with the development index. For example, the US – one of the most developed countries – ranks 33rd on the water index. Experts calculate that 20 per cent of world population in 30 countries faced water shortage in 2000 which would climb to 30 per cent in a total of 50 countries by 2025. The Earth Summit held in Johannesburg in September 2002, estimated that by 2015, half of the population of world will be without access to clean water and sanitation. Out of a total of 147 countries, the index ranks Finland at top, followed by Canada, Iceland, Norway, Guyana, Surinam, Austria, Ireland, Sweden and Switzerland and from bottom up are Haiti, Niger, Ethiopia, Eritrea, Malawi, Djibouti, Chad, Benin, Rwanda and Burundi.

Diminution of Natural Resources

The pattern of industrialization and development as is being pursued today has not only emanated substances to contaminate water and air due to which healthy and long human life has been threatened, but also caused imminence of the serious depletion of renewable and non-renewable resources. Energy is central to development process. Development, based on the modern technology, is impossible to continue without adequate availability of energy. Fuel and electricity constitute the most significant source of energy. It is only after achieving a considerable level of development that the significance of sustainable source of energy could be realized. Therefore, the concept of sustainable development, which began with the concern of people to innovate and develop renewable energy for development work as the non-renewable sources of energy like fossil fuel, would not sustain for long. Coal was the main source of energy in the beginning and it is in fixed stocks whatsoever under the earth which is sure to exhaust tomorrow or any other day. The need was, therefore, felt to base the developmental process on renewable energy.

There are several renewable resources on which the human lives are dependent – wholly or partly. Water, wood and plants are among such renewable natural resources. A perfect balance in ecology is needed for a healthy human life. Ecological balance is troubled when the renewable natural resources are exploited beyond their renewal rate and ecological imbalance also unleashes unhealthy conditions due to which the extent of renewability of natural resources is hindered. Thus, the over-consumption of resources causes depletion of the resources. Depletion of water is becoming a matter of great concern for the people today.

Depletion of Water

Water is one of the renewable natural resources. Consumed water is replenished by rains. But, the excessive use of water has created the problem of its depletion the world over. However, this depletion varies from country to country and from region to region according to the availability of water and pressure of population. The population growth is a serious cause of shortage of water today. The problem is grave in arid regions like North Africa and Middle East. In India, arid zones like Rajasthan are the areas of water depletion. The urban centres where there is high concentration of population leading to over-urbanization also suffer from the shortage of water. Quite a good number of people do not have access to palatable water in the big cities like Delhi and Mumbai.

Deforestation

There has also been excessive consumption of wood over the last few decades without being sensitive to dangers of shortage of trees. It has been used either for cooking or for furniture and decoration of houses. The innovation of advanced technology of felling trees accelerated the pace of decline of the forest area. Trees are the main source of oxygen on which depend both human and animal lives. Trees also help in rains. Jungles are the best protectors of animals and other creatures. Due to depletion of forests the rains have been affected and there has been (also likelihood of) extinction of several birds and animals. Poor rains affect the fertility of soil on which depends about one-third of the population of the world.

Global Warming

Global warming leaves great and threatening impact on earth's natural environment. Global warming refers to the rise of average temperature of the earth. The rise in temperature is a result of production of gases in greater quantities due to excessive human activities. Industrialization has also adversely affected the 'green house effect' as there has been excessive concentration of green house gases, particularly carbon dioxide, which has increased nearly 30 per cent since 1880 due to industrialization, deforestation, use of fossil fuels and emissions from vehicles and industries. Methane concentration has doubled and nitrous oxide concentrations are up too (Giddens, 2001). The result is that there is alarming rise in earth's temperature. Frantic use of refrigeration and air conditioning technologies has caused increase in chlorofluorocarbon (CFC), gases which is believed to cause depletion of the atmospheric ozone layer.

Politics of Environmental Pollution

Environmental pollution or ecological disorder is now a global phenomenon with regional variations in its nature and extent. Now, when there is anxiety and debate on this startling issue, countries are entangled in accusing one another for polluting the environment. The rich and powerful nations, which are the biggest consumer, hold that the poor countries are responsible for environmental pollution. Likewise, within a nation, the rich people hold the poor people responsible for pollution. The fact, however, is that the rich create pollution and the poor have to bear it. The rich contribute to pollution because they have enough money to enjoy consumption without facing its negative effect because, they can afford to counter the after-effects and also move away from the polluted area. Rich people's farm houses outside the polluted area of the city are common site whereas the poor in the city are usually found living in slums mostly located on the sides of railway tracks and roads.

Environmental pollution is directly linked with consumption level and living pattern. It is, therefore, also linked with the level of economic development and poverty. Pollution is the result of an unmanageable amount of residues and wastes due to the high consumption level, emissions from chimneys of industrial units, smoke from motor vehicles etc. This is an age of consumerism. Globalization has intensified it. This is a social reality involving both the affluent and the middle class, who can afford to go on replacing the consumer goods by the new ones as and when they are showcased in the market. The rich countries consume much more than the poor ones. They use large number of vehicles and are highly industrialized. The consumption level in developed as well as less developed world is increasing gradually. The consumption of fresh water has doubled since 1960 and over a period of 25 years, the consumption of wood has increased by 40 per cent. In the industrialized world, the wood consumption has been increasing 2.3 per cent annually. In East Asia, the rate has been 6.1 per cent. The richest 20 per cent of the world's population accounts for 86 per cent of private consumption expenditures, while the poorest 20 per cent account for only 1.3 per cent. The richest 10 per cent consume 58 per cent of total energy, 84 per cent of all paper, 45 per cent of all meat and fish and own 87 per cent of all the vehicles (see Giddens, 2001: 612).

Sociology of Environmental Damages

Environmental problem is a sociological issue and, therefore, a concern for sociologists to investigate and caution the world against the hazards entailed by development. People consume and generate waste to create the problem of garbage management, which includes its disposal and treatment. The higher the level of consumption, greater will be the use of technology and increase in production. Consumerism is rampant today and to meet the demands, production is not only augmented but also varied leading to excessive pressure on environment to accommodate with the challenges of development.

Consumption pattern is also a sociological reality. Except basic needs like hunger, thirst, sex and shelter, all other needs of people, which are innumerable, are socially determined. We buy many things essentially because others have bought them rather than we need them. Most of market commodities are considered the to be the determinants of social status and prestige. Many people may not necessarily need washing machines, cars etc., but try to buy them because others have bought them and these things confer a social status upon them. The rich consume much, use modern technology much and, therefore, damage the environment much, whereas the resultant offshoots of environmental damage are borne by the poor who are in no way responsible for it.

It is, therefore, suggested that people should be educated to cultivate a psychology of contentment and satisfaction which may be possible not by achieving more and more but by renouncing. Austerity, asceticism and renunciation are the only ultimate solution to the problem of environmental imbalance.

Remedial Measures

It is apparent from the above discussion that environmental degradation and depletion of natural resources are essentially a result of irresponsible extent and pattern of consumption, the present approach to development and cruel exploitation of natural resources.

Consumption is linked not only to the basic needs of the individual, it is also socially and economically conditioned. Consumption pattern of a rich person is quite different from that of a poor person because the former can afford many more things than the latter. A person buys certain things from the market not only because she/he can afford them but also because those things have been bought by others. In this age of consumerism, it has become fashionable to go on changing the items of personal use as and when the new items appear in the market. Consumption patterns have become an indicator of status of a person in society. People are engaged in a competition of conspicuous consumption.

The development, as is taking place today, is characterized by technological and commercial innovation oriented essentially to successive economic growth. As a result of this, there has been an unchecked use of modern technology in order to augment the quality and quantity of production. The modern efficient technology makes excessive production possible and over-production leads to over-consumption and consequently over-releasing of wastes and garbage causing environmental pollution. This is not all. Modern technology has introduced such domestic items as air-conditioner and refrigerator, which emit gases like chlorofluorocarbon (CFC), which react with the ozone gases leading to depletion of ozone layer and consequent ecological imbalance on earth.

The technology, based economic development has, no doubt, facilitated excessive production, but it has also led a capitalist economy. The monopolistic existence that the capitalist economy has succeeded in achieving has also created a market situation in which individuals and nations have entered into cut-throat competition and a new dynamics of power structure. A world system is claimed to have emerged, which is essentially a structure of hierarchical relationship between more developed and less developed economies of the world in which the central position is captured by the developed countries leaving the less developed ones on periphery. The world system will be discussed at length later in this volume.

A New Paradigm of Development

The old paradigm of development envisaged the active role of the government to ensure successive economic growth, removal or reduction of poverty, inequality, illiteracy etc. in the country. A citizen in the old pattern of development has been a passive recipient of the benefits extended by the government. The new paradigm of development has an orientation of reinforcing human values along with economic development. The relationship between the government and citizens should no longer be of an active giver and passive receiver but of co-travellers. The citizens will have full right to live a decent life and keep a watch on the functioning of the government.

On the basis of India's experience of development over four decades from 1950 to 1990, a new paradigm has been suggested by some Indian scholars who emphasize a shift in the role of the state and a greater interaction between the state and citizens. Arvind Virmani, in his proposal of the new paradigm, writes:

> The old paradigm of a moral, benevolent, omniscient and all-powerful state has failed. Though this paradigm had some validity in the mid of 20th century, post-war and newly independent India, it gradually lost its validity and reached a point at which it has become counter-productive. The deterioration in governance is broad-based and universal. Civic amenities, publicly provided utilities, public education and health law and order and justice have deteriorated at some places incredibly. Both availability and quality continue to decline.
>
> The proposed paradigm is as follows:
>
> Government's failure is now much more pervasive than market failure. Personal economic incentives are as, if not more, important than moral prescriptions or social strictures. In too many places government is part of the problem and not part of the solution. We must recognize the strength and weakness of the people and the state and allow and encourage each to play its role in economic and social development. To the extent the state has usurped the democratic rights/power of the citizens, power must be restored to the people and former made accountable to the latter. The view of the government as a 'milch-cow' or a 'mai-bap sarkar' must be replaced by a more self-reliant public that acts as a watchdog on the government. This paradigm sets three goals for the state to ensure: employment, entitlement and empowerment.

3 Theories of Development and Underdevelopment

Theories of Development

Stages of Economic Growth Theory

The theory of the stages of economic growth dominated the literature between the decades of 1950s and 1960s. According to this, economic development is a process which passes through different stages. This model is purely economic and, therefore, looks at problems of development purely from economic point of view. Development, according to this view, involves growth in savings, investment and foreign aid.

After 1960s, another approach proposed to analyze development was the structural-internationalist approach. This model views underdevelopment in terms of international and domestic power relationships. It tries to point out how the nature of development, as it is under process, brings different countries into the relationship of subordination and superordination. This is a people-oriented approach in which emphasis is essentially on locating the structural and institutional constraints existing in the path of development. This perspective defines development as a level of achievement of the objective of eradication of poverty, ensuring employment opportunities to the people, diversification of economic activities and reduction in social and economic inequalities. While the former approach concentrated on the production aspect of economy, the distribution aspect has become the focus of the latter one.

Theory of Economic Growth

As discussed in the preceding chapter, the classical economics treated development in terms of economic growth only. One of the most popular classical economists, W.A. Lewis considered the growth of per capita production as a symptom of development. Keynes presented a model of development, which emphasized that the rise in production level is important and it could be made possible only by raising savings and investment. Harrod-Domar also used the Keynesian model in measuring economic development. W.W. Rostow's book *The Stages of Economic Growth: A Non-Communist Manifesto* is perhaps the most famous work. Rostow's thesis is that economy must pass through a historical evolutionary sequence from traditional to the most developed mass consumption stage. Every society at a time must be at one of these stages. Following are the five stages of economic growth given by Rostow:

(a) Traditional society
(b) Pre-conditions for take off
(c) Self-sustaining growth
(d) Drive to maturity
(e) Stage of high mass consumption

This growth model represents the sequence of development experienced by the developed societies and the less developed countries must create a necessary pre-condition to take off to the self-sustaining economic development stage – the condition through which the advanced countries have passed.

The necessary pre-condition for development refers to society's increasing efficiency to promote savings and generate capital, develop managerial and entrepreneurial acumen of its people and make institutional and structural reforms to cope with new challenges of economic growth. Rostow's view is that when a society saves about 15 to 20 per cent of its Gross National Product (GNP), it is an ideal pre-condition for faster economic growth. But only saving and its investment is not enough for satisfactory economic take off, the important thing is that it should accompanied by efficient human capital, i.e., managerial and entrepreneurial skills.

Writing about the economic history of development, Karl Marx stated that the economy has passed through broadly three stages: slavery, feudalism and capitalism. These stages in fact represent transition of economy from agrarian to industrial, following the technological development. At every stage, there have been two classes: one, the class of those who possess and control the means of production and two, the class of those who are labourers and work for production.

Theory of Positivistic Development

Development does not mean merely a rate of growth in material gains and improvement in material standard of living but it also includes such social and cultural changes in the society which may facilitate material progress. The positivistic approach of development is a functionalist approach that concentrates only on the rules and processes determining the rate of development. It, however, does not visualize any conflict arising out of this development. The gainers and losers are not really the subject matter of this approach of understanding of development. There are mainly two sociologists namely, Auguste Comte and Talcott Parsons, whose views may be linked with the positivistic approach of development.

Comte writes about three fundamental stages a society has passed through in its historical evolution:

- Theological stage
- Metaphysical stage
- Positivistic stage

Historically, every society has passed systematically towards a society which believes more and more in the observable and verifiable facts. The progress of a society, according to Comte, lies in the achievement of a stage by that society where reliability of a reality is based on scientific understanding and it is verifiable. This is a modern materialistic world, which may be recognized as a progressive society.

Theory of Realistic Development

Till the beginning of the decade of 1950s, as we observed, the approach to development focused on production of goods without taking into consideration the distribution of production among people. Least was the concern about who received or who really needed the product. The United Nations Organization (UNO) also proposed that a developing country would be treated so only when it records 5 to 7 per cent annual economic growth.

But, the beginning of the second half of the 20th century witnessed an alternative approach to development, which focused on the distribution aspect of economy. This was a radical shift away from the idea of development conceived earlier. Development now started to be defined in, what we call, realistic terms that treat development as a composite concept consisting of economic, social, cultural and political dimensions. The approach became socialistic and welfare-oriented. Dudley Seers, questioning the preceding concept of development, gives a realistic definition of development. According to him, the questions to be asked about a country's development are: What has been happening to poverty? What has been happening to unemployment? What has been happening to inequality? If all three of these have declined from high levels, then, no doubt, this has been a period of development for the country concerned. If one or two of these central problems have been growing worse, especially if all three have, it would be strange to call it 'development' even if the per capita income doubles.

Theories of Underdevelopment

By the decade of seventies of the 20th century, the theory of the stages of economic growth became redundant and the structural internationalist theory became prominent. The structuralist approach looks at development in terms of the power relationship between different nations and between different people within the nation. The theory visualizes development as a process in which less developed countries are caught up in dependence and dominance relationship with rich countries and these subordinate countries suffer from institutional and structural constraints.

There are two views regarding how dependence of underprivileged countries upon the fortunate ones is treated as destined in the modern approach of economic development:

(a) One viewpoint is that not only the rich countries desire to have their hegemony over poor countries but also that the elite of a country, such as landlords, businessmen, bureaucrats, trade union leaders and entrepreneurs, support the sly intention of rich countries because they are rewarded for doing so. Todaro quotes a statement from *Theotonio Dos Santos of Latin America*, which is one of the most forceful statements regarding dependency nature of development:

> … Underdevelopment far from constituting a state of backwardness prior to capitalism is rather a consequence and a particular form of capitalist development known as dependent capitalism … dependence is a conditioning situation in which

the economies of one group of countries are conditioned by the development and expansion of others. A relationship of interdependence between two or more economies or between such economies and the world trading system becomes a dependent relationship when some countries can expand through self-impulsion while others, being in a dependent position can only expand as a reflection of the expansion of dominant countries which may have positive or negative effect on their immediate development. In either case the basic situation of dependence causes these countries to be both backward and exploited. Dominant countries are endowed with technological, commercial, capital and socio-political predominance over dependent countries.

(b) The other view that Todaro calls the "false paradigm" model is that the underdevelopment of the countries of Asia, Africa and Latin America is result of the inappropriate and faulty advice provided to them by the assisting agencies like UNESCO, ILO, UNDP, IMF etc. The intentions of the advisers may not be doubted as they are well-meaning experts but they are often ignorant of the existing situations of the target countries. The policies based on their meticulous expert advice prove inappropriate and reinforce the existing power structure and cater to the interests of powerful groups as these countries are beset with the acute problem of social, economic and landed inequalities.

Thus, both the views of structural internationalist model emphasize that the development would be more meaningful when the attention is drawn not only to the growth of GNP but rather to the planning of poverty reduction and employment to all.

The process of development is dualistic in nature. There are countries which have confined themselves to proceeding faster upon what has widely been accepted as the path of development and there are other countries which have not yet confined and refuse to move as fast as the former. These situations have naturally moved ahead to form dual societies: one treated as superior and the other inferior.

The theories of underdevelopment are essentially a dependency theories. This model relates to the scholars like Andre Gunder Frank, Samir Amin, Immanuel Wallerstein and H. Magdoff. Paul Baran, in his work *The Political Economy of Growth* (1973, first published in 1957), pioneered the theory of underdevelopment. This model views underdevelopment of the less developed countries as a consequence of the fact that the developed rich countries exercise dominance and imperialist assertion over the former. In his book *Dependency is Dead: Long Live Dependency and Class Struggle* written in 1974, Frank underlines the growth of class struggle between the rich and poor nations, which would aggravate due to aggressive policies of the former. Samir Amin's contributions *Class and Nations: Historically and in Current Crisis* (1979), *Crisis of Nationalism and Socialism* (1982), *De-linking: Towards a Polycentric World* (1990), *Euro-centrism* (1989) and *Mal-development: Anatomy of a Global Failure* (1990) are replete with evidences that bear out the role of rich countries in underdevelopment and backwardness of the colonial less developed countries of the world.

Modern economic history, as most of the social science literature, has been so written in the beginning as to establish the supremacy of the West. The Eurocentric interpretation asserts that the development of the Asian, African and Latin American countries is a result of positive contribution of the West. Indian and Chinese contributions to the development of Europe have been ignored. The other side of 'Europeanism' was 'orientalism', equally contemptuous of the non-Western world and, therefore, was criticized by Edward Said and Samir Amin (1989) in their writings against Eurocentrism. Europeanism is reflected even in the Marxist conceptualization of *The Asiatic Mode of Production*.

Baran's Views on Underdevelopment

Paul Baran is of the view that capitalism, due to its inherent characteristics, exploits the Third World. It is in the interest of the capitalist world to keep the backward world as an indispensable hinterland. These less developed countries were the source of raw material and extracting economic surplus for the rich countries. Most of the colonizers, according to Baran, were "rapidly determined to extract the largest possible gains from the host countries and to take their loot home" (1973: 274). Likewise, the per capita income, which is in paucity as compared to the rich countries, is a result of the capitalist development in the West. This economic stand off could be got rid of through socialist economic system. Baran was a promoter of the Marxist approach to economic planning. He believed that the existing class structure of the Third World countries has also been responsible for their dependent situation. The surplus of such countries was largely wasted, first by the 'lumpen-bourgeoisie' which included moneylenders, real estate agents and others who are considered to be non-productive and parasitic, and secondly by domestic industrial producers who were monopolistic, and belived in discouraging competition.

Baran is completely socialistic in his view and considers the present pattern of development to be capitalistic which is certainly exploitative. He wishes a society which is free from exploitation and that could be possible only in the socialist economy. Baran's obsession for the Soviet model of economic development forces one to consider him to be as utopian as Marx and Gandhi whose approaches have been possible to contemplate but impossible to implement.

The World System Theory

The important theorists associated with the world system theory are A.G. Frank, I. Wallerstein and S. Amin. Frank, inspired by the views of Baran, was the first to introduce the theory of world system and others followed with their own variant views. The common points among all the theorists are that they look at the history of the development of capitalism in the West and the economic relationship between the rich countries of Europe and the colonial poor ones. And, this relationship has been that of perpetual dependency of the latter on the former. There are four basic characteristics, which are common to all the theories of the world system:

1. There is a historical background of the capitalist world system consisting of developed and underdeveloped societies.
2. The world system consists of two extreme types of society along with an intermediary category.
3. There is an emphasis on international structure of inequalities ignoring the importance of the presence of internal socio-economic structures.
4. There is focus on unequal exchange between the rich and poor countries.

Frank's Theory of Underdevelopment

As stated above, Andre Gunder Frank was immensely influenced by Paul Baran. He, in the beginning, criticized the well-recognized contribution of Rostow's *The Stages of Economic Growth* published in 1971 and popularized the views of Baran.

Frank was very critical of the theories of sociology of development and connected processes of modernization and evolution. Hoselitz has used the Parsonian modernization pattern variables to explain the process of development in any country. Frank is convinced that neither developed nor undeveloped societies reveal the characteristics suggested by Hoselitz or, for that matter, by Parsons.

Frank also rejects the theory of diffusion, which suggests that the less developed societies cannot be developed because they are not able to be influenced by the changes in the developed world due to obstacles to development. Economic diffusions, according to Frank, do not bring about changes in the Third World.

Frank also criticizes McClelland (1961) and Hagen (1962). He is of the view that these scholars have ignored the fact that historical circumstances lead to the establishment of one world economic system in which the Third World functions to develop the First World.

Though Baran originated the theory of dependency but for its popularity the credit may be given to Frank. The basic elements of the theory of underdevelopment are:

1. Historical account of the underdeveloped societies.
2. Underdevelopment is a result of their relationship with the developed societies.
3. Development and underdevelopment are the two aspects of the same system.
4. Underdevelopment, dependency and world system are the names of the same theory.
5. This is a theory which presents a historical account of the relationship of dependency of the less developed countries on the rich European ones.

Frank is of the view that the world capitalist system involves both development and underdevelopment as the two aspects of the same system. Development in one area is a direct result of underdevelopment in some other area. Frank opines that the world system negates the significance of national boundaries and that countries are structured into the metropolitan-satellite relationship. This relationship is found not only between the rich metropolitan countries of the West and the poor satellite countries of the world but within a country too where the hinterland supplies to the city and is exploited by it. In the global economic system, according to Frank, metropolitan countries develop by expropriating the economic surpluses of the satellites and perpetuate their underdevelopment.

Frank has made a periodic presentation of the history of the world system. Both the processes of development and underdevelopment commenced in the mercantile period (1500–1770), carried through into industrial capitalism (1770–1870) and culminated in imperialism (1870–1930). Throughout the process, the colonies, semi-colonies and neo-colonies existed primarily for the benefit of the capitalist metropolis and as a direct result became underdeveloped.

Amin's Theory of Underdevelopment

The capitalism, according to Samir Amin, which was mercantile in the beginning, developed in the mid-19th century England and then became imperialist. In turn, pre-capitalist peripheral countries change from primitive communalism to tribute-paying societies and thence to capitalism (see Harrison, 1988). Amin writes: "Although this twofold process was accompanied by poverty and unemployment, it nevertheless represented and advanced in the development of the productive forces and the new socioeconomic equilibrium emerging from this process of transition to central capitalism was a higher equilibrium than that of the capitalist society that existed previously" (Amin, 1976: 204).

Amin divides the world systems into two sectors:

1. Self-centred systems
2. Peripheral systems

The countries which are self-centred have their own internal dynamic system unaffected by external relationships, whereas the countries on the periphery meet the requirements of the centre. Amin is of the view that the Third World countries are under direct influence of the capitalist world. Despite their own exclusive modes of production, these countries, under the influence of western capitalism, have almost similar capitalist nature of economy.

Wallerstein's Theory of World System

Immanuel Wallerstein is of the view that the modern world system followed the decline of feudal system and explains how the domination of Western Europe emerged between 1450 and 1670. The modern world system is essentially capitalist in nature. As against Frank's three stages, Wallerstein suggests four stages of the growth of capitalist world system: 1450–1640, 1650–1730, 1760–1917 and the period of consolidation after 1917. It is noteworthy that, for Wallerstein, capitalism as a system existed from the middle of the 15th century.

According to Wallerstein, feudalism was a dominant economy of the Western Europe between 1150 and 1300, which faced severe crisis during 1300–1450. In response to this crisis emerged the world economic system which encompassed most of the countries across national boundaries.

The capitalist world system is based on international division of labour. This division of labour determines the nature of relationship between different regions as well as the types of labour conditions within each region. Wallerstein divides the world into four categories of the regions consisting of a few countries. These categories are reflective of the political and economic characteristics and also the relative positions of the countries in the world system. The four categories are as follows:

The Core

During 1450–1670, the north-western Europe developed as the first core region. This region consisted of England, France and Holland. The states in this region developed strong governments and bureaucracies which helped them to have control over international commerce and extract surpluses from this trade for their own benefit. As a result of the crisis of feudalism, the peasants who were rendered landless and had to migrate to cities, provided cheap labour for urban industry which helped its development.

The Periphery

The countries put in this category are the East European countries (especially Poland) and Latin America. These countries lacked their own strong governments and were controlled by other states. They exported raw material to the core region. They extracted much of the capital surpluses of these countries through migrant exchange. The labour in this region was forced and made to provide cheaper raw material to be exported to Europe.

Semi-periphery

This region lies between the core and the periphery regions. It consists of the countries of the core region which are facing decline in their economy and those of the periphery whose economy is improving. Wallerstein cites the example of Portugal and Spain, which slipped from their core position to that of semi-peripheries. The core exploited the semi-periphery, which exploited the peripheries.

External Areas

These are the areas which maintain their own economic system. The internal trade is given importance by the countries of this region. Russia is the best example of this region.

Salient Features of Wallerstein's World System

It is the capitalist world economy. In this economy, the core region benefited the most and the periphery suffered the most but it is not that everybody in the core region became richer and that everybody in the periphery become poorer. The capitalist economy has intensified disparities. The kind of development the world has been passing through has widened social and economic disparities rather than prosperity to all (these views of

Wallerstein have been downloaded from internet "summary of his book *Modern History Source Book*").

World System Perspective and India

The main criticism labelled against the world system thesis of Wallerstein is that it is highly Eurocentric. He, like Marx and Weber, has asserted the western development model. In 1980 Frank Perlin criticized the world system perspective for its assumption that interaction between the West and the East was a one-way process culminating in incorporation and subordination of the latter, whereas the case of East India Company in pre-colonial India was different. Perlin identifies parallels between India's late pre-colonial history and the contemporary European history (see Currie, 1996: 91–92). K.N. Chaudhari (1985), following the lines of Perlin, asserted that metropolitan trading centres could not influence the decisions of producing units in India as sole agents. Nonetheless, these units were part of the 'world economy' with an epicentre in Surat, Ahmedabad, Agra or Lahore. Both Perlin and Chaudhari have concluded that the 17th century economy of Asia, including India, did not confirm the epistemology and Dumont's conviction that there was no concept of economy in traditional India.

Theory of Unequal Exchange

The most significant contribution to the situation of unequal exchange is that of Arghiri Emmanuel. Everyone knows that there is unequal trading relationship between the rich developed and the poor underdeveloped countries. But, more importantly, the theory of unequal exchange focuses on the reasons behind this unequal exchange. Unequal exchange is the most elementary transfer mechanism due to which there is uneven development and asymmetrical trading relationship in which the rich countries are the dominant ones. The basic point in his theory is that the labour is not as mobile across countries as the capital is. The natural consequence of this is that the wages of labour in the West are not as low as in the less developed countries. Due to lower rates of wages, the products in the less developed countries are cheaper than those produced by the developed western countries. Thus, the Third World is encouraged to produce more for export.

Dilemmas of Development

The processes of development, as we have passed through so far, have brought about some dilemmatic situations in which the nations are caught up and exposed to uncertainties regarding their policies of reforms and development. Technological revolution has taken place to give a fillip to economic development, sufficient modernization has taken place to make people quite rational and economically-oriented and wealth has increased and the standard of living has improved. But, the other side of the process is too glaring to ignore. Unemployment has increased, the gap between the rich and the poor has increased, globalization has increased and clashes of identities have also increased.

S.C. Dube (1996) has recognized four dilemmas of development, which have been debated and nations are in a puzzle while making choice between them. The dilemmas are:

(a) development vs non-development
(b) indigenous development vs foreign development
(c) self-sufficiency vs interdependence
(d) growth vs distribution

Development vs Non-Development

The offshoots of technological advancement and economic development have disenchanted some people and nations leading them to disapprove development and stay with non-development. The development has been seen as the great threat to human beings. Environmental imbalance and depletion of renewable natural resources, as are being faced in the world today, are the matters of great concern. Some scholars did advocate staying away from development but perhaps the human society is now unable to retreat from modernization and development. However, underdevelopment may not be a solution to the dangers of development. The cure is more dangerous than the disease. In order to ensure the human face of development and make the fruits of development available to all, governments will have to intervene and development cannot be left free to go on its own way.

Native vs Foreign

It is interesting to note the paradox today that where capitalist market economy is bringing nations much closer to one another under one roof and ensuing globalization is demolishing the national boundaries to allow free movement of capital, labour and commodities across national boundaries, a new and more jubilant and euphoric insurgence of the psyche of national, religious, cultural and linguistic identities is witnessed the world over. The normative principles of modernization have been exposed to ironical exigencies. For example, there is purely rational action of individuals in the market economy but the action of individuals oriented towards religious and communal and national objectives is irrational. People in India are quite educated but the fact that a section of them overlooks history and follows scriptural texts irrationally and blindly to relocate Indian history, geography and culture, is incongruous indeed.

Indigenous culture is hard to perish. It persists and continues to serve to define the identity of a person. The onslaught of globalization has not been able to eliminate individual cultures. However, the outbreak of culture and ethnic clashes, as have sprouted out of the fear of loss of identity, is unfortunate and quite worrisome.

Yet another dilemmatic situation today is to choose between development and sustainable development. This dilemma is more gripping in the less developed countries than the developed ones because the latter have already achieved the target of development by using those technologies which are now considered dangerous for the health of natural environment, whereas the less developed countries have yet to achieve the target of joining the class of the so-called developed countries.

Self-sufficiency vs Interdependence

This is the third dilemma. Any country and community would like to be self-sufficient. The bigger countries, due to their vast natural resources and raw material, claim greater self-sufficiency than the smaller countries which generally lack in natural wealth. India and China have always longed for self-sufficiency and economic independence. In pre-industrial rural communities, self-sufficiency was to some extent possible. But, in the modern economy with the shape it has taken, the concept of self-sufficiency is a misnomer. Almost all the countries which are striving for development have to be in the relationship of interdependence with some countries for capital, labour, technology, commodity, know-how and entrepreneurship. India provides know-how and labour to the developed countries and in exchange receives capital. However, the relationship of interdependence is not free from the element of dominance. The developed countries, which extend financial help to the less developed countries, also exercise considerable degree of authority over the recipients and force them to concede to their terms and conditions, causing their under development.

Production vs Distribution

Though this dilemma no longer holds significance as it has at least theoretically been accepted by the economists as well as the states that the uppermost concern of the state should be the distribution of production and not the production itself. We have already discussed earlier the paradigmatic shift in the concept of development. This shift has been from production to distribution. Distribution is targeted to ensure equality or reduce inequality in society. But, this has also remained only a utopian exercise. Judicious distribution of production is next to impossible in a country.

The capitalist economy, which is perhaps emerging as an unchallenged economy of the world, particularly after the demise of the USSR and the act of liberalization in socialist economies, due to its nature, is bound to promote cut-throat competition among the players in the economy, whether they are the capitalists or the workers, and ignore any judicious distribution of production. Inequality is bound to increase and it is evident today. Globalization has indeed raised the standard of living of people but at the same time the gap in economic status between individuals and between nations has widened.

4 Paths and Agencies of Development

Before the Third World countries moved, as independent nations, on the path of development, two broad models of development existed in the world: the capitalist and the socialist. These two mutually opposed economic models also had respectively the corresponding two political models: the democracy and the communism. Of the countries becoming independent, some followed capitalist model whereas some others went with a socialist one. Broadly speaking, the countries of Eastern Europe, Middle East and China, which were under the direct influence of USSR, followed the socialist economy and those of South Asia and South-East Asia went for the capitalist economy. This classification must be taken only as a tentative mapping exercise.

The Capitalist Path

In a country that pursues the capitalist model of development, every citizen enjoys complete freedom to take up the economic activity of his or her own choice. It is an economy of laissez faire. The capital is fully controlled by individuals. There is private ownership of the enterprise. It is also called the market economy because what goods and services and in what quantity and at what prices should be bought and sold are determined only by the buyers and sellers in the society. The market governs the rule of law of economic activities and determines the nature and direction of the economy relatively independent of state intervention. The nature and extent of jobs, wages, prices, production and distribution are essentially determined by market forces. The United States of America, the countries of the Western Europe and Asian countries like Japan and Sri Lanka are among the countries which have democratic system of polity and pursue the capitalist model of development.

However, citizens' autonomy of taking decision about their economic activity and the indifference of state towards the movement of capital is not absolute. No state can afford to remain indifferent to the needs and welfare of its citizens. Capitalism and unbridled governance of market forces has its own vices, for example, concentration of economic power, alienation of workers and smaller capitalists, widening gap between the haves and have-nots and the venerable situation of workers and consumers. Therefore, the state has to intervene in most of the economic activities without slashing the democratic and constitutional rights of the people in order to safeguard their interests and play the role of a watchdog. The state keeps an eye on the prices of commodities, sanctions a minimum wage for workers, and ensures judicious distribution of the produce and so on. Even the most developed capitalist and democratic economies like the USA and the Western Europe are not completely free from state intervention.

The Socialist Path

The socialist economy is a fully state-controlled economy. Capital is under the control of the state. It is an absolutely planned economy in which production and distribution are carried out under the dictates of the state. Socialist model is a welfare-oriented model and plans and attempts an equitable distribution of economic opportunities and benefits among its citizens with a view to reducing gap between the rich and the poor. Socialist economy is based on the Marxist ideology which believes in the principle of receiving from people according to their capability and giving them according to their needs. The then USSR, China, and the countries of Eastern Europe have been the communist countries and pursued the socialist path of economic development.

The capitalist and socialist economies are ideal-typical systems which never existed strictly distinct from each other and in true sense of the term. The distinction between the two may be made according to the nature and extent to which the economy is controlled by the state. It is interesting to note that after the depression of the 1930s and the Second World War, there has hardly been a government which left the economic forces in the country to operate freely without some measures of state regulation. The democratic countries control the economy by institution of laws and regulations and fiscal measures, leaving people otherwise free to enter into economic ventures, whereas the socialist countries have full control on capital and decisions regarding investment while leaving very little freedom to people to take economic decisions themselves.

The Mixed Path

The Third World countries, which were poor and undeveloped and in most cases had colonial history, after the Second World War, became independent one after the other, had before them two opposite paths of economic development, namely, the capitalist and the socialist, already in practice by the first and the second world, respectively. These countries were ideologically committed to a representative democracy and to the improvement of the lot of the common people. They chose one of these economies according to their existing social, political and economic circumstances. Some of the countries, including India, planned to have both the state and private entrepreneurs. Under the stewardship of the first Prime Minister, Jawaharlal Nehru, India, keeping in view the then social and economic conditions of its people, as resulting from subjugation to the British rule for a period of about two and a half centuries, opted a path, which was a combination of both the styles of economic development: the capitalist and the socialist. This is known as "mixed economy". In this economic system, certain industrial sectors of production and services are under direct control of the state and the other sectors of production are left free for individual investors and entrepreneurs. The first is known as "public sector" and the second, "private sector". There is also a third sector of industrial production, which is called "joint sector". This sector consists of those industrial units which are controlled jointly by the state and the individual investors.

Globalization of Capitalist Model

Till the early 80s there was a tri-polar world: the First World (comprising the American and Western European democratic countries), the Second World (comprising the USSR, China and East European communist countries) and the Third World (comprising the countries of Asia, Africa and South America, which were under colonial rule). These countries, after becoming independent, chose one of the prevailing economies. Thus, the nature of economy and the polity was clearly defined and compartmentalized. Since the latter half of the 80s of the last century, a radical change in economy and polity took place, which blurred the clean categories of the two opposite economies – capitalist and socialist. The supremacy of the capitalist economy made its hegemonic inroads even in strong socialist economies and is gradually displacing them. There appears a global influence and acceptance of the capitalist form of economy. The USSR (after disintegration) and China, the two leading socialist societies, opened their boundaries for foreign direct investment and started to liberalize their economic policies. India too, since the beginning of 90s, reformed its economy under the influence of the capitalist world. The process of globalization, naturally the capitalist one, started in a big way. The states started to liberalize, privatize and globalize their economies. This economic process dismantled the boundaries between these three economic systems of the three groups of countries of the world paving the way for a uni-polar world. It is a modern capitalist world system which, according to Wallerstein, has now emerged.

Gandhian Path of Development

The Gandhian perspective of development, for analytical purposes, needs to be located in the general theoretical framework of humanist and moralist social philosophy which Gandhiji not only spoke about but also practised. His points of view are rooted in his faith in truth and non-violence. Before considering Gandhiji's approach to economic development, we must keep in mind the fact that Gandhiji, while proposing his model of development of the country, was emotionally charged with a purpose of creating nationalist fervour and, therefore, his approach to development was more humanist and nationalist than purely economic. Therefore, Gandhiji's views may disappoint those who have only rational economic laws in mind.

Gandhiji detested 'industrial civilization' and advocated for 'handicraft civilization'. According to him, true Indian civilization lives in the Indian village. The industrial civilization, which is city civilization of Europe and America and of a few cities of India, cannot last long. It is only the handicraft civilization which will endure and stand the test of time. Gandhiji envisioned the revival of the village and in 1936 he said, "The revival of the village is possible only when it is no more exploited. Industrialization on a mass scale will necessarily lead to passive or active exploitation of the villagers as the problems of competition and marketing come in. Therefore, we have to concentrate on the village being self-contained".

Gandhiji was not against the use of modern machines in the handicraft industry so long as these were used not as a means of exploitation of others and the villagers can afford to use them. He was against the machines and technology, which render most of people out of work and are under the control of a handful of people. Machine makes large-scale production possible to be destroyed later on as is done by America. Production should be to the extent of fulfilling the needs of the poor and machine should be such that it may be controlled and used by all. Gandhiji was in fact not so much against the use of machines and big industries as the elimination of handicraft and cottage industries, which were the backbone of the Indian masses.

There appears to be a contradiction in Gandhiji's perspective. Gandhiji did not want people to remain as frogs in the well or follow the industrial civilization as it had developed in Europe. Because he was convinced that the evils of industrial civilization are imminent in the system to infest any society that adopts it. People know the offshoots of industrial development in the form of threat to the existence of family structure, village community, reduction in the number of people active in economically gainful activities, joblessness etc.

However, in his later thinking, Gandhiji seems to have relented to the need of use of machinery in manufacturing work but only to the extent so that it may be used by every artisan in the handicraft and cottage industries. He was against the use of machines to such an extent that majority of labourers are rendered jobless because elimination of poverty lies in the fact that everyone is working. Gandhiji wanted a peculiar combination of handicraft and machine. This combination of mind and hand may bring real life to the poor people of society.

Agencies of Development

The basic difference between development and change is that change may take place automatically and its pattern and direction may be different depending upon existing conditions, whereas development is a process that is planned and targeted and there are the necessary efforts are made to achieve that target. Development, as we have discussed earlier, refers to the process of betterment in the human life, increase in economic achievement and standard of living of people. This goal may not be achieved by an individual or a community alone. There is need of the support of some agencies in order to achieve this goal. There are mainly three agencies, which are recognized as playing active and positive role in development: the state, the market, and the non-governmental organizations.

State and Development

The state (the government) plays a central role in the development process of a country. Though the cultural and structural conditions are the preconditions for development, the role of state is uppermost because the industrial climate and necessary support are motivating forces for individual actors in society to move forward on the path of development. Despite the existence of high level of entrepreneurial acumen and achievement motivation, the supply of entrepreneurs and their entry into the field of business will not be possible unless the economic policies and programmes of the government are friendly and encouraging.

The role of the state is crucial not only in economic development but also in the social and political development of a country. The states, most of which are democratic and welfare-oriented, intend to ensure social justice in society by reducing inequality, promoting literacy, making health services available to all, and reducing infant mortality, birth rate and death rate. The following are the measures which the state in India has taken to bring about development in the country.

Economic Policy of the State

The state decides the priorities and the direction of pursuing economic activities in the country. The extent and nature of economic development depends on how the government plans and targets its economic achievements.

If we look at the history of economic planning of India, we would find two major economic regimes in the country. With the first regime, which began with India's independence, India began its self-rule with the philosophy of mixed economy – an economy consisting of both public and private sectors. Public sector refers to the industrial sector in which the capital and ownership are under the direct control of the government. The private sector consists of the industrial units in which investments are made by individual entrepreneurs. The idea behind reserving certain industries for the control of state was to thwart concentration of economic power in the hands of few and to provide jobs to the common people. Industries related with health, strategic and security considerations and so on were taken under the control of the government. The public sector industries were established by the government on a no-profit-no-loss basis and were aimed at providing maximum possible jobs to every section of the society. Through reservation policy, the Indian government tried to provide jobs, first to the scheduled castes and then to the other backward classes, with a view to improving their social and economic status.

The government, by the end of the decade of eighties of the last century, realized that the economic regime of 1950 to 1990 did not yield good results. Over the whole period, the annual growth rate had never been more than 3 to 4 per cent. Many public sector industrial units had become sick or were on the verge of closure.

After 1991, the government started to promote privatization to gradually reduce the magnitude of public sector. The disinvestments have now been undertaken by the government itself. The socialist parties, however, are consistently opposing disinvestments. Today, there are only five items which are under the purview of industrial licensing. Coal and lignite and mineral oils were also removed from the list of industries reserved for the public sector.

The policy of liberalization, adopted by the government in 1991, has contributed significantly to the growth of entrepreneurship and international trade. Where there were only 1 million small-scale manufacturing units by around 1990, the number rose to about 3 million by 2000. Red-tapism has ended and individuals have been relieved of the hassle of running from one office or table to another and still not getting the work done without greasing the hands of officials.

The role of the state is paramount in respect of the welfare of the workers in particular and citizens of the country in general. With the turn of the 1980s, we have been observing a radical and irreversible process of globalization. The government has now emphasized the need for privatization and liberalization of the economy in order to promote economic growth. The ideology of socialism, long-cherished by the USSR, collapsed under the hegemonic expansion of capitalism in the world leading to an end of the balance of power of nations. The capitalist economy has now strengthened and it characterizes the world system. The market rule now governs the economic as well as social behaviour of people. A major consequence of this depolarization of the world is that the Government of India, which, ever since it attained independence, had pursued the philosophy of mixed economy, maintaining a perfect balance between private and public sectors, has now liberalized the trade and the industrial policy. The purpose of having public sector undertakings was socialistic and welfare-oriented. The new economic policy of 1991 has lifted restrictions on trade and provided freedom to individual investors to a great extent.

Industrial Policies of Government of India

Industries (Development and Regulation) Act, 1951

The Industries (Development and Regulation) Act, 1951 was passed to implement the Industrial Policy Resolution of 1948. The provisions of the Act were that no new industrial unit be established or the existing one expanded without licence given by the Central Government. The government would take into account the location, size and risks etc. before giving licence to install an industrial unit.

Continuing with the policy of mixed economy, Indian government strived in every successive industrial policy to promote private investment but no significant entry could ever be experienced due to economic and bureaucratic constraints. The public sector also did not perform satisfactorily ever. The government announced new industrial licensing policy in 1970, industrial policy in 1973 and another licensing policy in 1975. Through the 1975 licensing policy it tried to liberalize licensing procedure to promote entrepreneurship. In all, 21 industrial units were delicensed.

The 1977 Industrial Policy

The Janata government announced a New Industrial Policy on December 23, 1977. The policy statement reads as follows:

> Unemployment has increased, rural-urban disparities have widened and the rate of real investment has stagnated. The

> growth of industrial output has been no more than three to four per cent per annum on the average. The incidence of industrial sickness has become widespread and some of the major industries are worst affected. The pattern of industrial costs and prices has tended to be distorted and dispersal of industrial activity away from the larger urban concentrations has been very slow.

The main thrust of the New Industrial Policy was to promote small-scale industrial sector. Three categories of the small sector were made: (a) cottage and household industries, which provide self-employment on a wide scale; (b) tiny sector units, which had investment of not more than Rs.1 lakh and were situated in towns with less than 50,000 populations; and (c) small-scale industrial units with investment not more than Rs.10 lakh; and in ancillary not more than Rs.15 lakh in fixed capital. Previously, 180 items were reserved which the government increased to 807 items by May 1978. Also, Khadi and Village Industries Commission was revamped in order to enlarge its area of operation.

State and Education

The role of education in development is crucial as it is not that the research and discoveries are of paramount importance for the development of technology and communication, but education has a significant role in creating awareness, belief in values of modernity, progress and development.

The Indian state has shown its carefulness and seriousness regarding its interest in promoting education. From time to time, it has instituted commissions like Mudalliar Commission and Kothari Commission to make necessary suggestions for achieving this goal. Despite the seriousness of the government, it has not been possible to ensure 100 per cent enrolment or inclination towards enrolment and retention, i.e., a large number of students drop out before reaching senior secondary education.

Education is important for development is exemplified by the fact that the areas which are educationally backward have not shown eloquent and positive interest in genuine implementation of policies and programmes of development. Education makes people ready for implementation of the policies and programmes of the state. It also creates demand for the necessary infrastructure for development in the minds of people and also the need to understand necessary changes in the culture. The nature of education is determined and reformulated according to the demands of the growing economy. The modern economy, which is more knowledge-based, and computer and information technology form the necessary infrastructure for the economic activities of today. As a result of which different new courses, particularly of professional nature like information technology, computer and business and financial management, have now become popular and the conventional theoretical education has been pushed to the back seat in the universities and colleges.

The government, therefore, makes policies and programmes to promote education among people by providing assistance and opening new institutions for teaching the modern professional courses. The Indian government has neither proved successful nor shown any serious concern about quick expansion of education in the country. Despite the recommendation of the Kothari Commission for an expenditure of 6 per cent of GDP on education, the government is not bothering to spend more than 3 to 4 per cent. About 40 per cent of people in the country are still illiterate and about 80 per cent of the students enrolled at primary level drop out by the time they reach senior secondary level. The number of universities and colleges has increased significantly but the quality of education and infrastructural facilities in educational institutions have not improved properly. In 1857, there were only three universities in Bombay, Madras and Calcutta. In 1947, the number of universities rose to 19. And, from 1947 to 2005, the number of universities expanded to as many as 320.

Similarly, till 1947, there were only 500 colleges, which rose to 16,000 by the year 2005.

Polity and Development

The polity and political processes are very important in deciding the nature and pace of development. This depends on the nature of ideology the party in power pursues. We have already discussed how the Indian government pursued the ideology of socialism and established mixed economy in the beginning of its independent rule which continued till the end of 1980s and from the beginning of 1990s it has shown its disenchantment from socialism and started promoting private investment and public disinvestment.

Democracy is the best form of government from the development point of view. It provides every individual equal opportunity for his/her progress and guarantees freedom to everyone to take up any enterprise and activity of his/her choice. But state protection and security is also important for the development of entrepreneurship and economic development. Therefore, it is important for development that the government be stable. The instability of the government creates the feeling of insecurity in the minds of manufacturers and workers, traders and consumers. In spite of the privatization policy, the state continues to monitor prices of commodities and wages of workers so that they are not exploited by the economic players in the market.

Rudolph and Rudolph (1987) have attempted to find correlates between the nature of polity of the state and economic characteristics. In a democratic country, there are two competing sovereignties: state sovereignty and voter/citizen sovereignty. Heuristically, they use two polar type ideal concepts to represent these sovereignties: demand polity and command polity. The demand polity refers to the situation when the government's policies and programmes are for the short-term benefits of people. The allocations and welfare activities are carried out keeping elections in mind. The model of command polity refers to that political set-up in which allocations and distributions are oriented to the long-term goals and sustainable benefits to people. The role of the state in command politics is monopolistic and oligopolistic. In the existing world, both these polities are found in a mixed form to varying degrees.

Which one of the two polities is more viable and acceptable would be decided by our experiences and the conclusions arrived at by the scholars. Rudolph and Rudolph conclude that "the consumption and welfare expenditures that demand politics generates can improve the productivity of human capital and enhance legitimacy; the voter sovereignty that demand politics expresses can promote governability by enhancing the legitimacy and efficiency enabled by citizen and producer commitment" (ibid.: 211–14).

The command politics relates to the postponement theory, which believes in investment for ensuring future development at the cost of the present needs and necessities of the people. Amartya Sen has attempted to estimate the cost to present generations of postponement-oriented development efforts. For example, in China and Sri Lanka, where short-term policies directly benefiting the poor were more visible than they were in India, the average life span in the late 1960s was 69 years, compared with 52 in India. Sen, in asking how long it would have taken the Sri Lankan economy to reach an income level likely to support an average life span of 69 years if it had invested in capital formation and less in social expenditure, concludes that it would have taken somewhere between 58 and 152 years. This kind of estimate has given certain concreteness to the costs implicit in postponement theories (see Rudolph and Rudolph, 1987: 216; see also Sen, 1982 and 1983). The demand politics is preferable to command politics because the former takes care of welfare, social justices and immediate dire needs of the public – the voters.

Market and Development

Market refers to a set of buyers of the commodities made available for sale by producers. The commodities in the shopping centres may range from agricultural produce to the large number of goods manufactured in factories. In pre-industrial societies, the range of salable commodities was small and consisted of only grains, fruits and vegetables and other agricultural produce and some non-agricultural handicraft-based industrial goods. With the rise of innovative efforts, scientific and technological advancement and entrepreneurial supply, the range of commodities has expanded manifold. It now consists of a huge variety of food, fashion and cosmetics, health and hygiene, knowledge and technology etc.

Market and industry are complementary to each other. Each determines the nature of the other. Which commodity and to what magnitude and for what prices would be produced is determined by the nature of demand from potential buyers. The size of population and the purchasing power of the people albeit are largely the main determinants. Thus, given the availability of necessary infrastructural and financial requirements, the nature and extent of industrialization would largely depend on the existing market. It is because of this fact that the market research has developed as an important branch of academic interest in educational institutions. The market is conditioned by many factors, from socio-cultural to economic and environmental ones, which will be discussed in this section at a later stage.

This is perhaps an old view that the market determines the nature and extent of industrialization. Currently, it is observed that the entrepreneurs innovate to produce and make efforts to promote the existing production combining the factors of production in a new way and also try to create market for their products. Earlier, the market was an independent variable but today it is created by entrepreneurs by way of advertisements, allurements and adjustment with the purchasing capacity of the buyers.

Role of Market in Development

The role of market in development may be analyzed in terms of the following dimensions of market situation:

1. The class status of buyers
2. The caste status of buyers: Indian context
3. The educational status of buyers
4. The value orientation of buyers
5. Urbanism among buyers
6. The caste characteristics of buyers
7. The geographical location of buyers

At the very outset, it has to be clarified that the above categories overlap one another. Their inclusiveness is due to the causative influence of one on the other. It is, therefore, methodologically more fruitful to analyze market situation in a holistic perspective. Where basic needs of people are the same everywhere, most of other needs are diverse due to their conditioning by exigencies of the people. Therefore, there is no uniform pattern of markets in the world. The buyers who constitute the market are influenced by their class and caste positions, level of modernization and urbanization and geographical conditions. The needs and consumption pattern vary along these factors.

The market consists of an array of stratified class categories forming a pyramid-shaped structure in which highest class is the smallest group and the lowest one is the largest. The highest class enjoys very high purchasing power but forms a small market and the lowest class is the biggest group of consumers but it has the lowest power to purchase. Significant place is that of the middle class which consists of quite a good number of people and also has a considerably good purchasing power. It is a big consumerist class which plays a significant role in the nature of economic development. The nature of the market is largely determined by the middle class. The high purchasing power and the large number of buyers are the two most important factors, which determine the nature and magnitude of industrial production in a country.

Indian middle class constitutes about 35 per cent of the population of the country and it is expanding fast due to the rapid growth in non-agrarian economy, urbanization, industrialization and change in traditional class stratification system. It is a significant group that plays a positive role in development of the country not only because it provides huge market for the industrial goods but also a large group of efficient and competent labour class ranging from manual labourers to bureaucrats, technocrats and managers. India today is looked at by the international business community as one of the best markets of the world.

NGOs and Development

NGOs are voluntary organizations (VOs). These are popularly known as NGOs because they are free from governmental control in their functioning. They are democratic and open to all those wishing to become member of the organization voluntarily and serve the society. Therefore, they have assumed a significant space in civil society, which is fast emerging today due to the weakening of the state. NGO is a popular term, which has gained currency at global level and commands respect in society due to its welfare services in society. The organization does seek financial assistance from the government but it operates, at least theoretically, on its own principles and programmes (see Punalekar, 2004).

VOs are, in principle, open to voluntary membership. Any one may become member by choice and resign from the organization at one's own will. However, Edwin Masihi writes that "it is wrong to label such organizations as free-for-all in that anyone who seeks admission gets it on demand. On the contrary, these organizations have their own rule of eligibility for admission and only those who meet these eligibility norms are accepted as members, albeit with the approval of the existing members. In that sense, these organizations are voluntary in relative terms only" (Masihi, 2004).

History of NGOs in India

NGO have a long history in India. In the past, people in this country have been found to have provided help to others in trouble. Since centuries there exists the tradition of voluntary service to the needy and helpless in the country. In the beginning, these services were rendered by people motivated by their religious feelings. They believed that service to people would be the service to God and, therefore, would be a means to attain spiritual salvation and sometimes to atonement for any sinful act. Spirit of charity and altruism guided the voluntary action in the past, which had found expression in diverse forms even outside the formal established religious channels (see Punalekar, 2004: 33). Many people including rulers have trod the path of service to their fellow beings and adopted it as their life mission (ibid.).

Floods, fires, earthquakes, epidemic outbreaks and other kinds of calamities were the occasions which motivated people to voluntary help those who were trapped in disastrous situations. Community life was very strong and people were guided by the 'we' feeling and selflessness in extending their individual support. The help and support used to be individual, spontaneous and transitory. It is around the late 18th and early 19th century that associations and organizations were being formed to render such activities in a more organized and permanent profile (ibid.).

The reform movements of the 19th century were perhaps the first organized forms of voluntary action in the service of society. This was the period when the caste rigidities were strong, untouchability was in practice, and other social evils like child marriage, cursed status of widow's were prevalent in the Indian society against which voluntary organizations came forward to launch reform movements. These organizations were liberal and cut across caste and creed lines and worked purely as a liberal and secular body. "In the early years of 20th century, the religious fervour gave way to more rationalist principles. The birth of the Servants of India Society laid the foundation of secular voluntary action in India"(ibid.).

Gandhiji was immensely concerned with the problems and evils the people were beset with. He, along with his war against the British rule, wanted to eliminate the social evils and awaken the people of India to come out of the closed shell of the evil traditions like untouchability, caste segregation, subservience to the landholding castes and general backwardness. In order to achieve these goals, several VOs were formed under the influence of the ideals of Gandhiji. A few of them are Sewa, Eklavya, Disha etc., which were instituted in Gujarat and some others might have been formed in other states also.

A significant growth of NGOs started after India achieved independence. Democracy was established and people had started understanding the meaning of freedom of speech, the charm of equality and the value of humanity and brotherhood. Also, on the other hand, the government started planning for development and in this effort, launched inter alia the schemes of Community Development Programme and later on the Green Revolution. Over one million NGOs are pursuing their economically gainful activities. The achievements of the schemes were assessed were found to be unsuccessful in providing for the minimum necessary requirements and reducing the gap between the rich and the poor in rural areas, instead rather increasing it.

With independence also accelerated the processes of industrialization, urbanization, expansion of education, politicization and democratization and modernization. These processes awakened people to be sensitive to the existing inequalities like economic inequalities (landed inequality in particular), gender inequality, inhuman kind of social segregations like caste inequalities and untouchability, other social evils like child marriage, child labour, restriction on widow marriage and many other stigmas and taboos.

Industrialization and urbanization led to the emergence of the problems of rural-urban migration causing imbalance in the rural division of labour, over-urbanization of many cities with the expansion of slum and pavement dwellers, urban unemployment, pollution and depletion of natural resources. Consumerism and over-consumption are yet other serious problems of the present nature of development. Most of the cities of the world in general, and those of the less developed countries in particular, have the grievous problem of garbage disposal.

Thus, there are hundreds of problems which have emerged and sensitized the citizens to organize themselves to work for their solution either by their own personal contribution or by pressurizing the government to solve the problem. Thousands of NGOs have thus emerged in India making significant contributions to the processes of development of society. "These NGOs believe in the tasks of mobilizing and conscentization of the masses or their specific target groups – be they women, children, agricultural labourers, construction workers or the social castaways like widows, *devdasis* or undertrial prisoners. They believe sincerely in educating the people and preparing them for ongoing struggle. They believe in social awakening including legal literacy and confidence-building" (Punalekar, 2004: 41).

NGOs have gained importance now and are increasing in number very fast. Enhancement of their importance is the result of weakening of the role of state in upholding the welfare and well-being of its citizens and consequent development of the assertive role of civil society to ascertain social welfare and integration. More than half a million voluntary organizations would perhaps be working in the country.

Role of NGOs in Development

NGOs have immense role in bringing about social change and development and it is being experienced from different parts of the country. Development, as we have read earlier, is a multi-faceted process, which essentially involves the aggressive participation of the people that would not be possible unless they are educated, awakened and motivated. NGOs are taking up this job sportingly and successfully. The areas in which we witness active and appreciative role of NGOs are as follows:

1. The NGOs are active to promote education, particularly among that section of population, which has remained unbenefited or less benefited by the measures adopted by the government. The education of girls, and other deprived people, particularly the SCs and STs, has been their target objective.
2. Women are the other vulnerable section of society. Gender discrimination is a ubiquitous cultural reality. Girls are discriminated in the upbringing pattern in the family. Larger numbers of the undernourished are from amongst the girls. Retention of girls in schools is much less as compared to boys. Women are forced to work as housewife and denied participation in gainful economic activities outside homes. About three-fourths of the work done by women is unmonetized.
3. Since the second half of the preceding century started the change in the status of women with their active participation in political, social and economic activities, which

gained acceleration since the last quarter of the preceding century. More and more women started moving out of the four walls of their houses and involving themselves actively in the social sphere outside their homes. Important in this process has been the role of academicians and NGOs. The book *Women's Role in Economic Development* by Easter Boserup (1970) is the pioneering work in this direction. After a gap of few years, by 1978, a large number of works were published, particularly on the status of women in the Third World – where their position has been more vulnerable. The role of women voluntary organizations towards this cause has been marvellous. Sewa, Sathin, Eklavya, Disha, Environmental Action Group and Agrani Foundation etc. are some of the thousands of NGOs known for their role in development by creating awareness among people and interventions, if required.

4. The approach to development has been almost uniform world over at least in terms of the use of technology, magnitude of production, pattern of consumption and achievement of wealth. Both state and people were unaware or lackadaisical about the backwash of the nature of development pursued. The threat to the human life developed due to environmental pollution and imbalance and the depletion of natural resources as a consequence of the nature of development. Here, the role of NGOs is really noticeable and praiseworthy. Thousands of voluntary organizations are at work to awaken people and governments against environmental degradation and depletion of resources.
5. It is not that the development process has unleashed only environmental threats to the human existence but also many people are displaced due to developmental projects and are quite often not properly compensated and rehabilitated. The NGOs have a major role to play towards the cause of people's resettlement and are also performing commendable job in this direction. The projects like the construction of dams, road highways and railways have often made some sections of people, particularly in rural

areas, vulnerable and are displaced without being properly compensated.

6. NGOs are also rendering great service in restoring dignity to the deprived and discriminated sections of the people in the society like women suffering from gender discrimination, lower caste people suffering from caste segregation and the status of untouchable, racial and religious discriminations.

Voluntary organizations, working at both national and international levels, have earned praise for their services in societal development. These organizations are busy in creating awareness and zeal for participation in development projects. Ensuring humanism by fighting against human rights violations, social exclusions, domestic violence and others have been common objectives of the NGOs. Of late, these organizations are also entering the sector of economic well-being and standard of living. In the state of Uttar Pradesh, Agrani Foundation's Jan Suraksha Kranti (JSK) scheme of savings and life insurance is indeed a commendable effort in this direction.

5 Industrial Entrepreneurship

Entrepreneurship is not an old concept. The scholars paid attention to its significance only after the Second World War when they concentrated on the problems of development of the Third World. It was admitted by the scholars that the problems of development in the Third World were more non-economic than economic. The countries of Asia, Africa and Latin America had slow pace of development and the most significant reason for this state of affairs was the sluggish supply of entrepreneurship in these societies due to their traditional mindsets and insufficient pace of modernization. Entrepreneurship is central to industrial development and essentially a sociological reality as it emerges and develops only in a conducive socio-cultural milieu. Gunnar Myrdal advocated the need for reorientation of the conventional approach and development of a sociological approach. The post-World War experiences of development, learned from the Asian, African and Latin American countries, forced the scholars of different streams of social sciences to admit that the problems of development in these countries were essentially non-economic and led them to share a common platform to advance the study of economic sociology, the foundation of which was laid much earlier by Max Weber.

The classical economics provided no space for entrepreneurship as a crucial factor in development. The American economists did recognize the input of entrepreneurial ability to ensure the development of big corporations in the US. There is a clear distinction between an entrepreneur and a capitalist. An entrepreneur may also be a capitalist but a capitalist may not necessarily be an entrepreneur.

Definition of Entrepreneur

The entrepreneur initiates, organizes, manages and controls the affairs of a business unit. He is in the centre of industrial production system. He is the owner of the business unit and works with the profit motive. The maximization of profit depends on many factors, such as the capital output, quality of the product, demand of the product and the internal management. But above all it requires entrepreneurial skill in the producer.

Kilby examined various theories of entrepreneurship and called the effort of understanding entrepreneurship "hunting the Heffalump" (Heffalump is a large animal which, despite ingenious devices, could not be captured). Likewise, there has always been an unsuccessful search for source of dynamic entrepreneurial performance. Kilby has evaluated theories of entrepreneurship and suggested some principles on which some traps may be designed. However, the dictionary meaning of the term 'entrepreneur' is "the person, who organizes, manages and assumes the risks of a business". Originally, the term 'entrepreneur' in the French language was used to refer to a person engaged in a leading military operation. Cantillon was perhaps the first to use this concept. According to him, the essence of the function of an entrepreneur was to bear uncertainty.

Entrepreneur is a person who buys factor services at certain prices and sells them at uncertain prices in future. In the late 18th century, Nicolous Bandeau called the agricultural cultivator an entrepreneur and credited him with the essential characteristics of risk-taking and innovation. J.B. Say emphasized the role of entrepreneur in bringing together the factors of production and in taking the risk involved in the management of production. He attributes an extraordinary insight and imagination to the entrepreneur. By far, the most systematic definition of entrepreneurship was given by Joseph Schumpeter, which was later on promoted by his follower A.H. Cole. Schumpeter writes that the entrepreneur is an 'innovator' who is characterized by potentialities of doing new things or doing things in a new way. He is an economic leader with atavistic willpower and sets a 'creative response' to a situation and acts as a chief conducive factor in the process of economic development. Cole defines entrepreneurship as an integrated sequence of actions taken by an individual or a group operating for individual business units in a world characterized by a large measure of uncertainty. G.H. Evans says that entrepreneurs are persons who initiate, organize and control the affairs of business units that combine factors of production to supply goods and services, whether the business pertains to industry, trade or profession. Thus, the common points that all definitions of entrepreneurship have are that it involves a sufficient volume of risk and adventure in the business enterprise under perusal, bears ultimate authority of taking decisions and formulating policies regarding the business.

Innovation refers to the new idea, which is applied for economic purposes, either for bringing out new products or new combination of the factors of production in the process of production. The entrepreneurs are innovators because they conceive new products and techniques and go forward to make use of them. Fritz Redlich also followed the innovation thesis of Schumpeter.

But, the innovation thesis has now become idealistic in character as most of the entrepreneurs at the ground level are not innovators but only imitators or fabians. Yale Brozen, following the terminology of Clerence Danhof, mentioned four types of entrepreneurs:

1. *Innovating entrepreneurs:* They make aggressive assembling of information and have capacity for putting an attractive combination of factors of production.
2. *Imitative entrepreneurs:* They have readiness to adopt successful innovations used by the first group.
3. *Fabian entrepreneurs:* They are characterized by caution and skepticism but do imitate if they feel that the failure to do so would cause a decline in the relative position of the enterprise.
4. *Drone entrepreneurs:* They are characterized by refusal to make any change even at the cost of reduced returns in comparison to others.

Technological advancement, according to Brozen, is possible where innovative and imitative types of entrepreneurs are heavily supplied. The sluggishness of the last two types will frustrate the attempt to advance technology rapidly.

This is truer particularly in the case of less developed countries. Redlich himself finds the entrepreneurs of Indian subcontinent to be only imitators and warns them against mere copy and duplication of the American type as it would yield unexpected and detrimental results. There would hardly be a business leader in the Asian and African countries who is an innovator in the true Schumpeterian sense and perhaps none is visionary enough to strike out for previously unexplored territory. All are imitators and adaptors of experiences gained in the economically more advanced countries keeping in view the existing conditions of their own. The technology they apply is usually borrowed from abroad, the legal marking practices they employ are adaptations of those developed in advanced countries and often the commodities they produce and sell are selected because of the operation of 'demonstration effect' through which consumption of the more advanced countries becomes popularized and enters the general demand in developing countries. Subrahmanya, however, finds entrepreneurs of England more innovative, whatsoever, than their counterparts in India. Evans also rejects innovation as an essential criterion and defines entrepreneur as "the person or a group of persons in a firm whose function is to determine the kind of business that is to be conducted". The entrepreneur has to take decisions regarding: (a) the kinds of goods and services to be offered, (b) the value of these goods and services, and (c) the clientele to be served.

It must be borne in mind that the interaction that has advanced between industry and scientific laboratory by now and the growing multiplicity of market and industry-related research institutions have reduced the innovational requirements on the part of entrepreneurs. Laboratories and market research institutions innovate and explore for entrepreneurs only to employ them in their enterprises. The entrepreneur now is to be characterized as having a personality formed of strong will to achieve, courage and readiness to utilize resources to the best of capability, ability to arrange and manage the functioning of enterprise and ability to take risk.

The entrepreneur, however, is essentially concerned with small and medium industrial units. Coleman emphasizes this view and entrusts entrepreneurs with the responsibility of continuously adopting to small changes in the market, both for factors and products. Small enterprise in India is defined in terms of initial investment limit in plant and machinery and the limit is Rs 10 million (Planning Commission, 2001). Indian entrepreneurs, in most of the cases, are not even near this limit. Most of industrial units are tiny in terms of both size and turnover and work for large industrial enterprises. Most of the entrepreneurs here are mere imitators. They do not dare to carry out radical changes in enterprises. The external factors, particularly market competition and customer needs, were the major motivating factors for small-scale entrepreneurs to engage in innovations.

Salient Features of Entrepreneurs

The entrepreneurs' motivation for creative activity lies in their intense urge for self-realization. The following are some of the important characteristics of an entrepreneur:

(i) High need for achievement
(ii) Acquisitiveness
(iii) Self-confidence and autonomous personality
(iv) Non-dogmatic and non-conformist personality
(v) Aggressiveness and risk-bearing capability
(vi) Rationality and pragmatism
(vii) Creative and technical mind
(viii) Adaptability
(ix) Managerial skill and leadership qualities
(x) Administrative ability
(xi) Sound decision-making ability
(xii) High personal efficacy
(xiii) High commitment to the task

Entrepreneurship is Central to Development

The classical economics laid emphasis on economic and material factors like capital, technology, labour and saving for economic development and the focus of the developmental analysis centred around physical and economic conditions. As stated at the outset, it was only after the Second World War, when the attention of scholars shifted to the problems of development of the so-called Third World countries of Asia, Africa and Latin America. It was then realized that the problems of their development were essentially non-economic and the scholars were sensitized to dynamically look into the reality of the interface of economy and society. As a result of it, the concept of entrepreneurship as a socio-cultural category received currency for its overriding place in economic development. An entrepreneur, who is distinguished for having innovative mind and temperament and striking business acumen, is born in suitable social, economic and political structure and cultural milieu. Differential degree of entrepreneurial supply in different structural and cultural regions of the world is a testimony to this fact. The capital and labour, despite their availability in huge quantum, may perhaps not create sufficient conditions for economic progress unless they are in command of able entrepreneurs.

Economic development without industrialization and industrialization without the precondition of impressive entrepreneurial culture is just improbable. At no stage in the history of development, entrepreneurial acumen might have been absolutely missing. But this was not observed and realized till the first half of the 20th century. The role of entrepreneurship in economic development could be understood only when the experiences from developing countries were gathered. Economic development means growth in the volume of industrial output, improvement in the quality of products, manufacturing of new products, creation of demands and ensuring supply of products to the consumers. This all is actualized only by an entrepreneur, who has the ability and temperament to innovate new products or technology and is so concerned about his enterprise that he spends his nights sleeplessly. The most significant point in Schumpeter's theory of economic development is that the key role in economic development is performed by the entrepreneur and if economic development by this theoretical assertion, depends essentially on the extent of entrepreneurial supply and level of business acumen, a proper and meaningful analysis of economic development would positively be sociological rather than economic. The role of social and cultural factors in entrepreneurial development will be discussed in this chapter at a later stage.

Schumpeter puts the entire theory of economic development in a new way. The factors which spur an economy towards development are not economic but extra-economic, to be more precise, socio-historical. The most significant point in Schumpeter's theory, which we would like to isolate for purposes of analysis in hand, is the role played by entrepreneurs in economic development. Since economic development largely depends on the extent of entrepreneurial supply and the level of business acumen, a proper theory of economic development would be sociological, rather than economic. He was right to emphasize that economic development depended on the development of entrepreneurship and entrepreneurship depended on the level of achievement motivation.

What at the moment needs to be emphasized is that the economic development of a country is not necessarily a consequence of material and economic geniality, as is commonly asserted by chaste economists. Decisive in economic development perhaps are socio-cultural and politico-historical conditions which have regional specificity and varying nature of impact on economy. Sowell writes that the cultural advantages that enable some groups to advance faster and particularly from poverty to affluence need not necessarily have specific skills. The Chinese, who immigrated into South-East Asia or to the United States usually, had little to offer besides a monumental ability to work hard and longer, and to save their money. Even with groups who had useful job skills, such as the eastern European Jews who entered the garment industry in the United States, their greatest success came ultimately in other fields, using new skills acquired by education or experience. Attitudes and work habits are often more crucial and take longer time to be acquired than do specific skills. The Chinese aptitude for arduous work, demonstrated in numerous manual occupations in South-East Asia and the United States, readily produced scientists and mathematicians when the opportunities arose. But groups without such traits seldom choose science and mathematics as fields of study, even when they are financially able to reach the college or university level. Of German and Scotch-Irish immigrants to eastern United States, the Germans prospered and Scotch-Irish remained poverty-stricken despite the fact that the latter pioneered a little ahead of the former because of difference in their work habits. After World War II, the cities, ports, railroads, bridges, factories and power stations in Germany and Japan were reduced to heaps of rubble and ashes. What was left was the tradition of hard work and technical skill which brought them back as greater economic powers than before the war. Borrowing capital from advanced countries is not as important as to arrange knowledge and technology. What Japan and the erstwhile USSR borrowed from other countries was not so much the capital as technical know-how. The Japanese Emperor, at the advent of Meiji era, had declared that intellect and learning would be sought for throughout the world in order to establish the foundation of the empire. Stalin, during the First Five-Year Plan of the USSR, confessed that they did not intend to conceal the fact that in the sphere of technology they were the pupils of Germans and the English, the French, the Italians and mainly the Americans. Hagen (1971) and Rippy (1931) have observed that Columbia developed not for economic reasons. The inflow of foreign capital started in that country, in fact, after a sufficient degree of economic growth had taken place and attractive market had been established. Sabana and the valley regions of that country where there was concentration of growth were difficult places to reach. The growth in the area did not wait for the development of infrastructure and social overhead capital. Transportation and communication and power facilities developed as a result of the demands created by growing production rather than as a prior step which laid the basis for the latter.

Hagan is one of the foremost development theorists who emphasized the role of social factors in the process of economic development. His thesis is that entrepreneurs emerge from social tensions arising due to status crisis. On the basis of his observations carried out on the Samurai community of Meiji's Japan, he concludes that the status withdrawal of individuals in the course of historical changes led them to entrepreneurial plight. Although, Hagan's assumption has been questioned by Leonard Kasdan, his conclusions may not be rejected outrightly. The point that emerges from the foregoing discussion is that economic development is not so much a result of certain a priori economic conditions and favourable physical, social and cultural situations that exist in the background as it is an outcome of the level of entrepreneurial supply and growth of business acumen which is largely determined by these factors.

Approaches to the Study of Entrepreneurship

The concept of entrepreneurship as we have studied so far is not a very old one. It became a popular subject of study only after the Second World War, the time when the students of economic development concentrated on economic problems of the less developed countries and realized that the real problem of development in the less developed countries today is not as much economic as it is non-economic. The element of entrepreneurship in the process of industrialization and economic development could be realized as early as by the beginning of the 19th century. Weber and Schumpeter may be considered the first scholars to have systematically explained the role of entrepreneurs in productive enterprises. Since then, scholars of different disciplines have been concentrating on the issues like social, economic and political bases of entrepreneurial supply, psychological characteristics of entrepreneurs and entrepreneurial functions in the business enterprise. There are broadly four approaches to the study of entrepreneurship:

1. Sociological Approach
2. Psychological Approach
3. Political Approach
4. Composite Approach

Sociological Approach

The sociological approach to the study of entrepreneurship deals with social and cultural factors responsible for the nature and growth of entrepreneurship development in a society. It attempts to understand as to why a social structure and culture facilitates or inhibits entrepreneurial development. It believes that laws of development lie in the social structure and culture of a region. It tries to seek answer to the question, why one segment of social structure produces larger number of entrepreneurs than the other. For example, it is mainly the Samurai community that could rise to entrepreneurship during the Meiji regime in Japan. Indian entrepreneurship, from the very beginning, has been dominated by three communities: the Parsis, the Gujratis and the Marwaris. They, however, continue to dominate the business sector even today.

Max Weber, Cocharan, Young, Hoselitz and Hagen are prominent among the scholars known for sociological interpretation of entrepreneurial development. Max Weber's thesis is that Protestantism, and not Catholicism, could help generate entrepreneurship and modern capitalism. Weber believed that the Hindu religion of India did not have the potential to promote entrepreneurship. The traditional social structures; the caste and the joint family which were essential attributes of the Hindu society, according to Weber, have been detrimental to the process of entrepreneurial growth. Kapp (1963) also holds the Hindu culture and Hindu social organization responsible for slow pace of development and suggests that "a lasting solution of the problem can be found only by a gradual but systematic transformation of India's social system, world view and the level of personal aspirations".

The Parsonian model of development, best known as ideal-typical approach to entrepreneurship and development, relates to his popular schema of pattern variables. B.F. Hoselitz used the Parsonian model of pattern variables to explain how entrepreneurship development is a function of socio-cultural changes known as modernization. Hoselitz uses three of the five pattern alternatives given by Parsons which according to him are applicable to the problem of development: the choice between modalities of the social object (achievement vs ascription), the choice between types of value orientation standards (universalism vs particularism) and the definition of scope of interest in the object (specificity vs diffuseness).

The backward economies, according to Hoselitz, exhibit usually a lack of reliance on achievement as a norm for acquiring economic goods. Achievement-oriented behaviour is however not fully absent but exists only in limited cases. Distribution of economic goods in primitive societies and also in medieval societies has been typical example of ascriptive way of distribution pattern. The advanced societies, on the other hand, exhibit the norms of achievement-oriented behaviour. In such societies, there is system of formal education and vocational and professional training.

The second characteristic of underdeveloped economies is the prevalence of particularism in the distribution of economically relevant tasks among performers. Particularistic pattern of distribution has been prevalent, for example, in the traditional Indian caste system. The advanced societies have universalistic i.e., rational approach to the allocation of resources. Again, it is to be emphasized that both these variables do not exist in the respective societies in their pure forms. The movement of society is seen from particularistic to universalistic system as it moves from backward to advanced economy. Sir Henry Maine has also postulated this movement with different terminology and that is from 'status to contract'.

Thirdly, in the backward societies, economic activities are quite diffuse. It is so because of the fact that there is a low level of development of division of labour. Partly it is the result and, at the same time, cause of the low level of productivity. Thus, the specialization of tasks and the finer division of labour require the development of principle of specificity and rational allocation of roles. Specificity is the outcome of rational planning, the result of the combined application of the principles of universalism and achievement as the norm to economically relevant social situations. Hoselitz concludes that the analysis of social structural aspects of the differentiation between "advanced" and "underdeveloped" economies leads us to conclude that we expect the former to exhibit predominantly universalistic norms in determining the selection process for the attainment of economically relevant roles; that the roles themselves are functionally highly specific; that the predominant norms by which the selection process for those roles is regulated are based on the principle of achievement, or "performance". In an underdeveloped society, on the contrary, particularism, functional diffusion and the principle of ascription predominate as regulators of social structural relations especially in its economic aspects and the orientation of actors in economically or politically influential roles is determined predominantly by considerations of their ego.

Cocharan is of the view that entrepreneurial development depends to a substantial degree on cultural factors. According to him, patterns of child rearing and family life determine the personality patterns. Frank W. Young, in his 'Mediation Model' of entrepreneurial activity, points out that the entrepreneurial attributes show up in individuals as a result of particular family background and as a reflection of general cultural values. Entrepreneurial characteristics, such as the ability to make new combinations of factors of production, managerial skill perception of opportunity, risk-taking, inventiveness and achievement motivation are not merely a pale reflection of these antecedent conditions; they constitute an independent causal factor mediating between structural factors and consequent economic development.

E.E. Hagen opined that the traditional authoritarian social structure inhibits the growth of personality with entrepreneurial talent. His thesis is that an entrepreneur is a creative problem-solver with innovative temperament interested in things in the practical and technological realm and driven by a sense of duty to achieve. Modern democratic system is more conducive to the development of innovative behaviour. According to him, they are more prone to taking up entrepreneurship as a career whose existing social status has been denigrated in the course of historical change.

Psychological Approach

We have understood by now that the entrepreneur is not a common person. He has a typical personality with creative, managerial and imaginative skill who can innovate and contribute positively to an industrial project. This kind of personality develops in a person who has strong motivation for achievement. David McClelland, the greatest exponent of the psychological approach to entrepreneurship, is of the view that the genesis and performance of entrepreneurs requires strong motivation for achievement. The achievement motivation, according to McClelland, is a function of child rearing practices in a society. Unlike the sociological approach which asserts that the existing social structure determines entrepreneurship and economic development, the psychological approach seeks to find out how the social structure affects the attitude of the people of a society. Areas like entrepreneurial commitments, tendency of saving and investment and business management have been usually covered by the studies carried out by psychologists. Collins, Moore and others have examined a sub-category of business leaders. Their study of innovating entrepreneurs revealed that many of their subjects had experienced childhood poverty and disrupted family lives which stimulated strong motivations for personal achievements.

John H. Kunkel questioned the validity of many psycho-dynamic concepts and principles and the unresolved controversy surrounding the role of social structure and personality in the process of economic development. He propounds the behavioural approach as an alternative.

Joseph Schumpeter, the first to offer a systematic interpretation of entrepreneurship, had psychological perspective in his mind when he said that the entrepreneur possesses energy of will and mind to overcome fixed habits of thought and the capacity to withstand social opposition.

Political Approach

The political approach to entrepreneurship deals with the issues involved in relationships between entrepreneurship development and the state particularly in the context of the role of the latter in the development of entrepreneurs. The role of the government is crucial in deciding the nature and rate of development. Rapid growth of industries and good pace of economic development largely depend on the merit of economic policies of the government. Democratic and relatively stable governments are supposed to be conducive to economic development. Entrepreneurial supply would be greater in a state which believes in the ideology of capitalistic liberalism and provides requisite credit facility, appropriate training opportunity, technological and scientific knowledge and adequate incentive.

The Government of India pursued the policy of mixed economy till the end of 80s of the 20th century which could not contribute to growth rate of 3 to 4 per cent for over 40 years of the economic regime of the country. Corruption, laziness, traditional power structure and weak governance, responsible for sluggish development, could not be removed by the state.

Economic reforms initiated by India from 1991 with an objective to liberalize economic policies, promote individual investors and bring about structural adjustment have undoubtedly yielded significant results.

Entrepreneurial growth in India had been very slow till 1990. A long span of colonial rule and the following strict and partially controlled economy and red-tapism did not allow fast entrepreneurial growth. By 1990, the number of small-scale units in the country was about 10 lakh which, due to economic reform movement, swelled up to about 35 lakh by 2005. Political studies on entrepreneurship have revealed that the late growth of entrepreneurship in Russia and France had been due to the existing political conditions in the countries. Japan's fast entrepreneurial growth can be attributed to the country's political system which peculiarly integrated the industrial and agricultural economy. The role of state in development has also been discussed at length in the preceding chapter of this volume.

Composite Approach

As we have mentioned earlier in this chapter, entrepreneurship is a complex phenomenon. None of the approaches discussed above has been able to explain the entrepreneurial dynamics fully. Due to their non-holistic nature, they have failed to offer the precise laws of supply and success of entrepreneurship. It has been observed that entrepreneurial behaviour is an outcome of the interplay of multiple social, cultural, economic, political and psychological factors. No single factor is entirely responsible for the supply of successful entrepreneurs. We, in our study of carpet manufacturers in the Bhadohi-Mirjapur belt in India, found no manufacturer entering into business on account of any single factor. Dwijendra Tripathi also, in his comparative study of historical roots of industrial entrepreneurship in India and Japan, has observed that the emergence, performance and perception of entrepreneurs can be understood by an integrated approach which would take into account all the possible sociological, psychological, economic and political factors contributing to the increase in entrepreneurial behaviour. The variables like business acumen, motivation for achievement, modern and progressive value orientation, minimum necessary capital, technical knowledge, adequate market and favourable political conditions need to exist together for the development of a milieu conducive to entrepreneurial supply and industrial development.

Entrepreneurship Development in India

History of modern industrial production in India is not old but non-agricultural industrial production in country is really so. Handicrafts of artistic quality manufactured by the indigenous artisans occupied pride of place during the 17th and 18th centuries. Silk weaving in Varanasi, woollen shawls of Kashmir, stone carvings of Rajasthan and woolen carpets of Bhadohi-Mirjapur are some of the items that can quoted as examples. Rise of Indian entrepreneurship in India has been staggering. Political, social and cultural factors have been considered to be responsible for this state of affairs. Indian entrepreneurship, therefore, can be understood only by taking into account the broad historical conditions.

Non-agricultural Production in Traditional India

Although, factory-based industrial production in India started hardly a century ago, evidences prove that the non-agricultural manufacturing existed even during the Mughal period, which occupied place of excellence in the world. Highly skilled artisans of the country were engaged in manufacturing cotton textiles, means of transport (ship building in particular), house construction, metal and stone works. Cotton textile was mainly manufactured and produced in almost every part of the country.

Dacca, Patna, Banaras, Lahore, Multan and Allahabad were the places of repute for the fine quality cloth. Technology used for production was simple and cheap. Production was a household affair and its supply was confined to meeting the demands of people of the same village. The urban market was very small and only the remains of the production after village consumption were transported there.

Caste-based Organization of Production

In pre-colonial India, manufacturing was mainly a rural activity. Agriculture and non-agricultural manufacturing activities were organically linked with the caste-based social organization of the village to provide self-sufficiency to the village life. The manufacturing was carried out by the artisan castes. Artisan castes like weavers, potters, carpenters, blacksmiths and some lower caste with fixed hereditary occupations like barbers, grain-roasters, water-carriers and washermen used to serve the land-owning higher castes people. The service-providing occupational castes and service-receiving higher castes were traditionally tied with each other into a relationship of client-patron type. The former served the latter by their occupations which, in turn, provided shelter to them which included payments in kind (agricultural produce at the time of harvesting and a piece of land for their own cultivation). This socio-economic institution was called 'jajmani' system. The 'jajmani' system has been appreciated by functionalists like William Wiser and K. Ishwaran as a healthy rural economic system but the elements of dominance had been glaring in it. With the outbreak of market economy and urbanization, the jajmani system of economy started getting weaker day by day and by the end of the second quarter of twentieth century and with abolition of 'zamindari system', the jajmani system came to an end, though, some residual symptoms of the system continued for a few more following years. Ended also the customary relationship between landlords and the occupational castes serving them.

The artisans, who were usually from the lower castes, had very little opportunity for upward mobility. They were paid very low remuneration, that too, mostly in kind and had a modicum of living. This is one of the reasons why Indian artisans could not rise to become entrepreneurs as did the European counterparts after Industrial Revolution and urbanization.

Rise of Indian Entrepreneurial Class

Modern industrial activity in India started around the middle of the nineteenth century. It was a very modest beginning and most of manufacturers in the beginning were the British. Tata Iron and Steel Works was perhaps the first Indian enterprise to start in the year 1911. Cotton, jute and coal were the first fields which constituted the industrial sector. This was the time which marked the end of the dominance of the traditional industries and opening of the gate for the supply of indigenous entrepreneurship.

Journey of Indian industries began with cotton textile. The first cotton mill was established in the year 1854 by a member of the Parsi community – a successful cotton merchant of that time. Industrial growth in the country accelerated during the Second World War, but the emergence of entrepreneurs was very slow. Two major factors have been considered to be responsible for the poor entrepreneurial supply:

(a) Policies of the British Rule

(b) Indian social structure

The British administrators, after the Industrial Revolution in England, needed the Indian market to supply the finished goods produced in huge quantities by the machines and transport the raw material of the country to their factories. This was made possible by them by way of implementing the policies which discouraged indigenous industry. Therefore, the British administrators transported the raw material to Britain and discouraged indigenous manufacturing to allow the British products to find a market in India.

Apart from the British inhibitive industrial policies, the Indian social structure did not support the growth of entrepreneurs in the country. The caste-based traditional social structure had fixed occupation for each individual and provided very little liberty for occupational mobility. Traditional business caste people, due to their occupational heritage and training in business activities, entered entrepreneurial arena first. Other caste people could not pace with them in this field due to their non-conducive social background. The scheduled castes had and have the lowest representation in the business field.

The rise of Indian entrepreneurial class is marked by the entry into manufacturing sector initiated by the three communities of the country: the Parsis, the Gujaratis and the Marwaris. The probable reasons of such an entrepreneurial plight of these communities may be ascertained. These communities were initially traders and also did not occupy a clear-cut defined social position in the caste hierarchy. Gujaratis were the first after Parsis, to have entered the business field. These communities had a background of business family. The Parsis were ship-builders, The Gujaratis were the traders and the Marwaris had the background of moneylending. Gujaratis from the Hindu community were the first to enter the manufacturing field. Parsis and Marwaris were significant business communities during the period between 1911 and 1931. Indian society is marked by an assemblage of different castes and communities characterized by their specific social and occupational norms. These communities influenced the course of development in the country. It is because of this perhaps that the Indian entrepreneurship has always been numerically dominated by traditional trading castes. Over the last three decades, radical changes have taken place in the Indian social structure as a result of drastic urbanization and social and occupational mobility, which have contributed to significant entrepreneurial supply from the non-business castes of the country.

The scholars have also tried to analyze the sociological conditions which have played a role in entrepreneurial development in the country. Gadgil studied Indian entrepreneurship in the 17th and 18th centuries from historical perspective and concluded that the modern business class mostly came from the social communities that were traditionally involved in trading, finance and handicraft activities in different geographical areas. Lamb wrote that since the advent of factory system around the middle of the 19th century, the three Indian communities which entered the entrepreneurial field were the Marwaris, Gujaratis and Parsis. He also wrote that one is puzzled by the apparent contradistinction between the hierarchical view of society as contained in Indian caste system and the obvious vigour of Indian trading communities. Andrew Brimmer studied the impact of managing agency system on the setting up of entrepreneurship in India. James Berna, who studied 52 industrial installations in the then Madras State, found that the traditional social structure did not stand out as an obstruction in the process of entrepreneurial growth. His study shows that the entrepreneurs, contrary to general belief, do not preponderantly belong to the traditional group of traders with a traditional world view of economic activities and investment. Hazlehurst in his study of Ram Nagar tried to analyze the factors of caste and social community behind entrepreneurial activity. He pointed out that in the rise of entrepreneurs not only is there a structural continuity in the form of the old trading groups but also a break by way of the refugees, who, according to him, have played significant role in the process of economic experimentation with new consumer goods.

The entrepreneurial class has been closely related to the modern Indian economy and also it inherits the legacy of the past. In order to know the class character of Indian capitalists, it is essential to understand some important features of the evolution of modern Indian economy. Important to note is that the British imperial economic policy was imposed on India with the only objective to subject the Indian economy to the colonial market. The natural resources of the country were plundered and the indigenous productive forces, particularly the artisans and the skilled labourers were denied pursuance of their jobs and thus their talent was impeded.

The negative approach of the British did not allow Indian entrepreneurship to develop smoothly and satisfactorily. Though modern industrial production may be said to have begun around 1850 but two features were dominant: one, most of the industrial units were established by the British except a few which could be called truly Indian concerns; and two, the British imposed a new economic policy in India which had the objective of converting Indian economy into a colonial market by plundering its natural resources and obstructing the development of its indigenous productive forces. It is important to note that the British rulers invested much in the transport and communication sector though for their own economic requirements. The British industrialists built a well-knit network with the Indian business class which consisted of native importers and exporters, brokers, merchants, landlords and users. The native capitalists helped foreign ones in consolidating their economic interests in this country. As the network grew, the peasants and village artisans became impoverished. Gradually industrial bourgeoisie developed in India from merchants and moneylenders. However Indian bourgeoisies remained mostly trading partners than an industrial class. H. Venkatsubbiah, however, wrote in 1949 that Indian big bourgeoisie was a class which was yet in the early stage of emerging from a trading class into an industrial class. The surpluses from trading still provided substantial funds for the new industrialization.

The basic weakness with the Indian capitalists became apparent at the end of the colonial rule in India. The means of production required for the development of industry were virtually absent. Except for very meagre production of iron and steel, coal and a few chemicals etc., the articles of productive consumption were hardly produced in India.

Significant changes have taken place in recent years in the socio-economic composition of the entrepreneurial class of India. Before independence, only the big bourgeoisie monopolized the industrial arena of the country. The Indian government followed the path of planned development and made efforts to expand the socio-economic space of entrepreneurship, but for over four decades of planned development, the numerical strength of the very small, tiny and village industries in the country has been high.

The economic reforms started by the Indian government since 1991 have indeed brought out a new economic regime in which the policy of promoting liberalization, privatization and globalization has been contributing to expand the social space of entrepreneurial supply, increase the number of industrial units and swell the magnitude of industrial production. Today, the Indian industrial sector is quite significantly represented by a cross-section of castes and classes but continued poor representation of the scheduled castes in the field is also a truth. Therefore, important to note is not that which castes are taking up entrepreneurship, but the fact that the scheduled castes have been denied opportunities and continue to lag behind.

Industrialization in India

The steam-powered machines started operating quite early in India and elsewhere in South Asia and the pace of its extension was quite fast. Between 1850 and 1914, major industries were established in the country. Production of jute and cotton textiles was enormous and the railway network was as extensive as to have the third place in the world. These conditions had guided

Karl Marx to be optimistic that India would soon become a crucial and leading economy of the subcontinent. But why was it so that after almost hundred years of optimistic industrial conditions, the country remained non-industrialized and one of the world's poorest at the time of independence, is a big question which has sought the attention of intellectuals. The answer to this question lies in the following:

(a) The country was under colonial rule in which industrial venture was essentially of the British. Money, mind and management were those of the aliens who introduced industrial machines, made their revolutionary use in England and brought them to India for their own manufacturing enterprises. Railway network was established by them for their own use. Thus, the entrepreneurship, machines and infrastructures were essentially of the rulers and were meant to help them to appropriate their business interests.

(b) The British policy inhibited local initiative and discouraged the emergence of indigenous entrepreneurship. They exploited the local markets and raw materials. The existing conditions also did not help the development of industrial economy. The pace of investment was very slow. It depended upon the local value system and social structure. The rate of investment was low also because the cost of production was high and the opportunities were bleak.

(c) The caste structure and traditional outlook of the people inhibited entrepreneurial supply. Occupations of most of the people were hereditary and change of occupation was restricted. Modernization and urbanization had not set in till then and education level was pathetically low.

(d) The population of the country was large but due to the fact that the per capita income was very low and much of this income was generated in the non-monetized activities, the investment was highly restricted. It is interesting to note the estimate of Phyllis Deane that in 1750 the per capita income of England was three times that of the average Indian in the early 1950s.

(e) The traditional non-agricultural industries, such as stone carving, ivory work, carpet weaving, handloom work and many other handicraft works, were mostly luxury goods which had the scope of a small market. The princely states and zamindars were the only buyers of these products. This aristocratic class was a miniscule population and could not continue to sustain their status at a later stage. The luxury goods had thus a small market which due to their decline shrunk still smaller causing serious crises to the artisans by way of making their skill meaningless and rendering them to the modicum level of living.

(f) The nature of demand was one of the major factors to influence entrepreneurial supply. India's population, at the beginning of 19th century was about 200 million which swelled to 417 million by 1947. But due to very low average per capita income, this enormous population could not necessitate introduction of machinery and modern technology. Most of the activities of the people were unmonetized.

(g) The supply of machinery and modern technology to India was also inhibited because of the fact that due to underdeveloped condition of the country, most of the factors of production were costly, machinery had to be imported and human capital was mostly unskilled and fuel and domestic transport was costly.

Though the first industrial unit, which may be said to have been established by an Indian, was TISCO in the year 1911, but the momentum of industrialization in the country started only after independence when the country could plan its industrial development.

India's Industrial Growth

We shall be discussing in this section the small-scale industrial (SSI) sector development in the country mainly for two reasons:

(i) entrepreneurship, the subject this chapter is concerned with is essentially related to SSI; and

(ii) SSI sector is one of the most vital sectors of the Indian economy in terms of employment generation, the strong entrepreneurial base it helps to create and its share in production.

Small-Scale Industries (SSIs)

An industrial undertaking is graded as small-scale industrial undertaking in which the investment in fixed assets in plant and machinery, whether held on ownership terms, on lease or on hire purchase, does not exceed Rs 10 million.

As the economy improved, the Government of India raised the investment limit and thus redefined the SSI sector. For example, in the year 1970, the investment limit in SSI was only 7.5 lakh which was raised to 10 lakh in 1975, 20 lakh in 1980, 35 lakh in 1885, 60 lakh in 1991 and 300 lakh in 1997. It was brought down to 100 lakh in 1999, which continues till date. Likewise, investment limit in 'tiny industrial unit' in the year 1977 was 1 lakh which has risen to 25 lakh.

A small-scale industrial unit/industry-related service or business enterprise, managed by one or more women entrepreneurs in proprietary concerns, or in which she/they individually or jointly have a share capital of not less than 51 per cent has been treated by the government as a women's enterprise. Women entrepreneurship enjoys special benefits from the government.

The small-scale industry sector has been India's engine of growth and continues to be so in the new millennium. By the end of March 2000, the SSI sector accounted for nearly 40 per cent of gross value of output in the manufacturing sector and 35 per cent of total exports from the country. Through over 32 lakh units that exist, the sector provided employment to about 18 million people.

The office of the Development Commissioner (SSI) has till date conducted three censuses of registered SSI units. The first census was conducted in 1973–74 and found 2.58 lakh units registered up to 30 November, 1973. The reference year for this census was the calendar year 1972. During this census, only 1.4 lakh units were found working. The second census was conducted during 1989–91and was found that 9.87 lakh units were registered up to 31 March, 1988. The reference year for this census was 1987–88. During this census, only 5.82 lakh units were found working. The Third All-India Census was conducted during 2002–03 and it was found that 22.62 units were registered up to 31 March, 2001. The reference year for this census was 2001–02. During this census, only 13.75 lakh units were found working.

It is significant to note that the entrepreneurial supply to India, as is apparent from the above statistics, has been sluggish. In a period of forty years since independence, the country could produce only six lakh successful entrepreneurs. It is only after India adopted the New Economic Reforms in 1991 that the supply of entrepreneurs gathered momentum. Thus the speedy growth of entrepreneurship in the country may be attributed to mainly two conditions:

- Economic Reforms Policy, 1990, which liberalized the industrial policy by doing away with the compulsory cumbersome licensing system and making trade practices easier.
- Cumulative impact of urbanization and modernization processes in the country.

6 Structure, Culture and Development

Processes of development are not independent of the existing social, political and cultural conditions of society. Social structure plays a crucial role, both positively and negatively, in determining the nature and extent of development. Development largely depends upon the compatibility of the cultural and structural conditions of society. Durkheim's holistic approach to understand society, undermining the identity of the individual, does not help us understand the principle of the development as we conceive it today. Predominance of conformism, societal cohesiveness and collective consciousness inhibits emergence of leadership traits and entrepreneurial acumen among individuals. Weberian thesis, on the contrary, helps us understand the fact that the culture has a great role to play in the nature and extent of economic development in a society. Weber's thesis attempts to prove that it is the

Protestantism and not the Catholicism, which has led to the development of modern capitalism in Europe.

The early economists rejected the idea of social and cultural influence on economic growth. They treated economic variables as the only crucial factors in development. The experiences of the development the world over have forced us to realize the need to have a theory that would relate economic development to cultural development. The facts that Jews have excelled at others, Samurais have outstripped other Japanese and Marwaris, Gujaratis and Parsis of India have not only pioneered but also dominated the country's industrial sector, are enough to prove that social structure and culture have a great role to play in economic development.

Among scholars, there has been an inconclusive debate regarding compatibility and incompatibility of specific social and cultural factors with reference to development but the consensus among them has been on the fact that they are largely responsible for the supply and performance of entrepreneurship. The sluggish development in the country, despite no dearth of natural and human resources, has triggered fervent debate on Indian entrepreneurship. Western writers have held that Indian social and cultural conditions have not been conducive to entrepreneurial growth. Value orientation and entrepreneurial aptitude have been treated by the scholars as correlates. Hindus, Jains and Catholics have been observed as not having as much zeal for business activity as the Protestants. The role expectations and social sanctions as prevail in a society also determine the nature of entrepreneurial growth.

Weber's thesis, based on case studies of different religions, does not necessarily correspond to existential situations and, because of its failure to apply universally, has been challenged by Samuelson. In India, Jains and Banias (traditional business castes) are leading entrepreneurs and are also commonly found to be quite religious and ritual observing. Even Brahmins, positioned at the top in traditional caste hierarchy and supposedly most conscious of ascetic values, have shown keen interest in entrepreneurial ventures.

The western thinkers like Weber had expressed a very negative view about the prospects of Indian economy. Indian social institutions and the social structure, for them, have been great inhibitors in the path of economic development. Indian caste system, joint family system, religion and rituals and superstitions hinder entrepreneurial growth in the country. Their assertion reveals their failure to understand the Indian society which presents a peculiar blend of history, society and culture of the country. Caste system as a cultural phenomenon, Hindu religion as an orthodox cultural reality, several superstitions and many other cultural conditions have been taken as the factors responsible for the slothful entrepreneurial development. The caste, it has been asserted, has not been conducive due to its cultural dimension. It had tied occupations with religion imposing restrictions regarding occupational mobility on caste members. Also, the status of a person was determined by the measure of occupation on the scale of tradition-modern dichotomy. Mobility in traditional Indian society had never been completely impermissible; even in medieval period, instances of social and occupational mobility did were there.

Cultural differences are economically important in respect of the attitudes and stereotypes formed regarding the nature of work. And, this would have its far-reaching impact on the nature of entrepreneurial supply. It was a taboo for the upper-caste men to handle plough in the field and equally tabooed was the use of grain grinder by the upper-caste women. Many whites in societies in which blacks were enslaved came to associate hard, manual or menial labour with the race to which they felt superior. There were found sayings among whites that "work is for Negroes and dogs". They had a feeling in colonial South Africa that it was "shame to work with hands". These notions had a great role to play in entrepreneurial supply. Even the best enterprising West Indian blacks in the United States have long had a distinct aversion for manual labour. The non-trading castes of India were prohibited to go across sea to do business. Certain elements of Indian culture did not prove conducive to economic development. The philosophy that the pleasure and pain being experienced by a person in this life are a result of the acts of that person carried out in the previous life and the glorification of carrying out of acts only selflessly and the ideal of renouncing everything, would never create a culture that would promote entrepreneurial aptitude among the people of a society, which cherished this philosophy as India did. Yes, such values, if cherished in society, would no doubt be a sufficient reason for poor economic performance. But none of the cultural values discussed above have ever been so unyielding that it would have its deterministic role in inhibited entrepreneurial development.

The western views about the Indian scenario of entrepreneurial surfacing and performance may be blamed for being narrow and eurocentric. Fatalism, superstition and status quoism are not the particularistic features of Indian society as has been the notion of western writers. Western societies also, like any traditional society, must have been fatalist, superstitious and status quoist before Industrial Revolution, Renaissance and modernization and have not completely shed them even today after having achieved the pinnacle of economic development and urbanization. But, their tradition of structural and cultural values was not as deep as that of India and, therefore, it did not refuse to give in to new values. Indian social structure and culture, due to the fathomless depth of their roots and multiplicity of their dimensions, on the contrary, did not allow new values supposed to be conducive to entrepreneurial growth and economic development.

While discussing the low productivity of labour in the developing countries like India, the western social scientists have opined that the workers in these societies, due to their primordial attachment and loyalty to such institutions, like family, caste and religion, have less commitment to industrial performance.

The knowledge of the link between economic development and the nature of social system is possible only through Parsons' 'pattern variables'. The pattern variables are the choices between behaviour patterns of individuals which determine their nature. These variables as sociological foundations may help understand the development and underdevelopment of a society. B.F. Hoselitz has used Parsons' pattern variables to explain the role of social system in development. Parsons points out five pattern variables, i.e., the choices between alternative normative behaviour patterns prevailing in a social system which determine the extent of development in a society. The pattern variables of Parsons reduce the distinction between economically advanced and economically less advanced economies to its basic sociological foundation. These pattern variables are the sociological categories, which are regarded as determinants of the nature and extent of economic development. Of the five pattern variables, Hoselitz utilizes the following three, which relate to different levels of development:

1. achievement vs ascription
2. universalism vs particularism
3. specificity vs diffuseness

Achievement vs Ascription

Economically backward societies usually exhibit lack of the norm of achievement for acquiring economic goods. Primitive societies in which kinship relations, i.e., ascriptive rather than achieved statuses, determine the pattern of distribution of goods, are the best examples of this kind. The undeveloped traditional societies assign statuses to its people by birth. People in such societies normally do not strive for achievement. The lack of attitude of achievement negates emergence of entrepreneurship and developmental environment in a society.

Achievement, on the other hand, is the normative behaviour pattern, which prevails in economically advanced societies. The developed societies, particularly Western European ones and the USA, did not have as closed structures and occupationally and socially ascription-based system as many South Asian and less developed countries had.

Particularistic vs Universalistic

The second pattern variable, i.e., particularistic vs universalistic normative pattern, also relates itself with the underdeveloped and developed economies respectively. Economic roles and economic results in underdeveloped economies are distributed on the basis of particularistic principles whereas in the developed economies, universalistic principles are followed in the distribution system. Ascription and particularism are well-known normative patterns in primitive societies. Sir Henry Maine observed that the "movement of the progressive societies has hitherto been a movement from status to contract". This proposition is conveyed in the fact that the ascription and particularism get transformed into achievement and universalism as the given society advances from an underdeveloped to a developed economic status.

Specificity vs Diffuseness

Thirdly, specificity and diffuseness are the two other binary approaches a society follows on the principle of achievement and universalism to the allotment of roles in the advanced economies. Specificity is concerned with the allotment of roles to a specific person who has earned knowledge and skill. The advanced economies have high degree of division of labour in which economic performance is specifically allotted. Thus, the job is kept open to all who may compete among themselves to grab the job. This is individualism in true sense of the term based on the norm of achievement.

In the primitive societies, on the other hand, the allotment of economic roles is fixed according to traditionally assigned statuses to the people in the social structure. Thus, specificity is not absent in undeveloped societies. The allotment of roles in primitive societies is also specific but not to a person who has acquired skill for that role but a person who has traditionally ascribed a particular status. In advanced societies specificity is coupled with achievement and universalism whereas in economically backward societies specificity is coupled with ascriptive and particularistic values.

According to Hoselitz, the three pattern alternatives must be seen in combination to explain the contrast between economically advanced and underdeveloped societies. They are not simple descriptive symbols but a part of functionally related framework. We may conclude from the Parsonian parameters that a society moves on the path of development if it honours statuses achieved by individuals not bestowed upon them by birth, assigns economic roles to individuals who deserve and not the one specifically decided by tradition and honours universalistic principles.

Caste and Development

If the pattern variables of Parsons discussed above are applied to the Indian caste system, it is obvious to conclude that the traditional caste system was beset with such structural and cultural characteristics which did not help development in India if they did not inhibit it. However, it is not easy to deny the fact that the traditional caste system with specificity, particularism, ascription and hereditary occupation as its basic values had its stronghold in the country when it was economically backward. With the economic advancement, as it has taken place in the country, it is observed that most of the traditional caste characteristics have withered away.

What role has the caste played in the development process of India needs a careful scrutiny. Some scholars have taken caste system as a major inhibitor of development. Max Weber holds it responsible for India's economic backwardness. As we know, the choice of occupation was not open, the caste used to choose occupation for its members. The occupational mobility was almost nil. Among the higher castes, certain manual economic work was tabooed. The status of an individual was determined by the status of family and the status of families varied from caste to caste. Thus, the individual had neither freedom nor motivation for achievement.

James Berna's study on entrepreneurs of Madras State, on the other hand, concludes that caste has no role to play in entrepreneurship development. He found that entrepreneurs hailed from different caste groups.

It is not so simple to understand the role caste played or is playing in economic development. This objective may not be achieved without a foolproof methodology. A close scrutiny reveals that caste did play a detrimental role in the process of entrepreneurial development but the fact that must be taken into consideration is that it is not so much the culture as much the structure of caste that contributed negatively to the process. The salient features of the traditional caste system, which inhibited the development, are discussed as follows:

Hereditary Occupation

The caste system provided little freedom to its members to choose occupation of their own choice. Most of the castes had fixed occupation for its people which passed on to the next generation in the family. Most of these occupational castes had lower status in the caste hierarchy. On the other hand, there was no clearly defined occupation for higher castes. Normally, the people of higher castes had only supervisory role and they considered manual work a taboo. In such a normative condition, occupational mobility was terribly limited and the work culture was impaired.

Ingressive Personality

The traditional caste system attached many social and economic stigmas to a significant size of the population of the society in which some were treated as untouchable. The caste structure existed parallel to the class structure in the Indian society in which the landed property was so distributed that lower the caste, smaller was the land size, rendering the lowest castes almost landless. The lower caste people, who were subjected to social and economic inabilities and denied decent status in the society for centuries, were shaped in such a way, which would not be suitable for entrepreneurial development. An entrepreneur has aggressive personality and leadership qualities which may not develop in a person who has remained under subjugation for long. The scheduled castes and the marginalized backward castes, therefore, have not been able to make their presence in the manufacturing sector in the country.

Jajmani System

The rural economy of India was caste-based. The caste decided the division of labour. There were landowning higher castes and a large number of landless or small landholder lower castes. The lower castes included mainly occupational or artisan castes. The artisan castes, like washerman, potter, barber etc., served the higher castes and received only protection in returns. They were not paid any remuneration in cash for their services. Though Wiser and Ishwaran have eulogized *jajmani* system as a good economy of mutual confidence and trust but the *jajmani* kind of economy was essentially exploitative. Payment to the serving castes was made only in kind and that too only seasonally. Both the serving and the served castes were bound to depend on each other for generations. Gough and Kolenda have argued that the *jajmani* system was essentially dominating and exploitative. The artisan caste people in India always lived a modicum of living without any cash in their hands. Artisans in Europe did not suffer as much as their counterparts in India because they were not trapped in a *jajmani* kind of economy based on caste system. As a result of this, European artisans were not as poor as the Indian ones. Therefore, during the Industrial Revolution, the artisans of Europe became entrepreneurs while their Indian counterparts could become only industrial workers. This is all because of the fact that entrepreneurship, apart from leadership and aggressive personality, also requires a minimum capital for having confidence in making innovation and the Indian artisans, due to *jajmani* kind of economic system, could not.

Entrepreneurship is a composite phenomenon. Entrepreneurial personality, suitable cultural and structural milieu and the congenial industrial environment created by the government and certain amount of capital to initiate the effort are in combination decisive in entrepreneurial and economic development.

Family Pattern and Development

The joint family system has always been a point of debate in the context of economic development. The discourse is based on whether joint family system is beneficial or detrimental in the process of economic development.

While discussing the concept of joint family, one must be careful about the definition of joint family in order to stay away from any misapprehension of the linkages between joint family system and economic development. It should be kept in our mind that traditional joint family was not a mere assembly of persons of three or more than three generations. The normative aspects of joint family were really important and significant from the point of view of entrepreneurship development. The following were the core characteristics in the joint family of traditional India:

1. The structure of family was authoritarian in which the eldest male member enjoyed the ultimate authority. The status of women was lamentably low with complete denial of their participation in economically gainful economic activities. Their life activity confined within the four walls of their houses.
2. The property was essentially landed and common and customarily and legally less divisible.
3. The members of the family were of several generations and morally bound by rights and duties.
4. The size of the household was usually large.

We find mixed views regarding linkage between joint family system and development. Statistics related with entrepreneurial development in India do not confirm that entrepreneurial development is hampered by joint family system. D.R. Gadgil, S.D. Mehta, R.C. Fox, M. Mines and T.A. Timberg have instead found that the joint family system is strengthened by entrepreneurship. However, their findings may not correspond to every section of entrepreneurial supply as they studied only traditional business communities. A.D. Ross, M.S. Gore and K. Davis are of the view that industrialization leads to the development of the pattern of nuclear family whereas I.P. Desai writes that there is a cyclical change in the family organization. J.P. Murdock is of the opinion that family has great adaptability to the challenges of changes in the society. Michael M. Ames finds that there is predominance of joint families among the workers of the steel city of Jamshedpur.

Processes of development and urbanization bring about drastic change in the nature of joint family such as rule of residence, forms of marriage and authority system.

Agriculturist, upper and middle, classes have mostly joint families whereas urban professional families are nuclear ones.

David McClelland, in his book *The Achieving Society,* writes that the studies of child rearing practices show that among others, the early training of children to be independent and to master certain skills promotes high motivation for achievement, that training does not indicate rejection of the child by the parents. McClelland concludes that the children of authoritarian fathers show low achievement whereas fathers of high achievers are found to be generally loving, affectionate and less dominating.

Entrepreneurship and modern capitalism could develop more among Protestants than Catholics only because of, as Weber claims, the fact that Calvinism promotes rational economic activity and entrepreneurial aptitude. The population growth and capital accumulation together can explain only a small part of the growth rate in the countries that have moved forward rapidly in the last couple of centuries. Hagen's study of Samurais of Meiji Japan highlights the importance of the socio-psychological approach to understand economic development. Weber, Hagen, Cocharan, Young, Hoselitz and Myrdal have confirmed the crucial role of social and cultural factors in the growth of entrepreneurship and accelerated rate of economic development. In Japan, values of family allegiance are strong and extend even to industrial sector providing a family environment in business organizations. This has helped Japan's manufacturing sector compete with any country of the world. The countries with higher level of educational achievement have recorded much faster rate of development than the countries or states of a country with lower level of educational achievement. That is why, China, Japan and Sri Lanka have performed better than India. McClelland's thesis that entrepreneurial personality consists of high achievement motivation and this develops in a person as a result of suitable child rearing practice. This kind of socialization process takes place in a family, which features small size, democratic structure and urban traits. That is why, perhaps, at least in India, entrepreneurship still is essentially an urban phenomenon. Nearer to this observation is the French entrepreneurship, which is largely elitist. The elite professional schools of France, as has been observed, fetch candidates from bourgeois families and the graduates from these schools prove to be arrogant due to which not only personnel relations in the organization become difficult to manage but they do not care for the mass market as well.

Gender and Development

Woman is centripetal in the development economics but has remained centrifugalized by a universal culture of gender discrimination. The labour of a major section of working women has been devalued, unpaid and hence unaccounted for by the proponents of economic growth model. A significant portion of women's activities carried out, as part of their familial obligations, do not enter the market place and fetch income and, therefore, are excluded from GNP estimates. The unmonetization of work of a large number of men and women causes a significant loss to the economy of a country. The Human Development Report, 1995, of the UN records a loss of about $16 trillion to the global economy due to unmonetized work. Of this sum, only women's share is only about $11 trillion whereas women work harder and for a longer period of time than men. Women have been marginalized by planners by treating them as passive beneficiaries of social and health services. Their active and productive roles in their societies were neither recognized nor included explicitly in development planning.

It is not easy to understand the role of women in the development process of India. The status of women as housewives has been ubiquitous, but the nature and magnitude of economic activities rendered by them vary from one section of people to another. Indian society is a caste society. Traditionally, caste used to choose occupation for its members, define their lifestyle and family norms and determine their socio-economic position. The status of women here also varies from caste to caste. Economic position of women should be interpreted in terms of their participation in economic activities. Women of high castes performed duties of housewives only and were not allowed to carry out any work outside the four walls of the house. The middle and lower caste women, on the other hand, had full participation in economic activities of the family in addition to their duties as housewives. In traditional India, the cottage industry and agriculture were intertwined to form a composite village economy and, in both the sectors, women had full participation. But their contribution to the objective production results has never been treated as their own share not even nationally. This denial of economic right to women in the family is a culturally determined reality.

Traditionally fixed cultural boundaries of roles and economic activities on the lines of sexual discrimination are now being challenged by women the world over and no longer are the workplaces, earlier meant for only men, a prohibited zone for women. But this progress at least in India is only a trivial phenomenon. This varies from one region or section of society to the other. Gainful economic activity by a woman outside home is still essentially an urban phenomenon.

Entry of women in manufacturing sector is only a recent development, which reflects radical cultural change and occupational modernization. Industrial entrepreneurship is a gender-neutral concept. Woman entrepreneurship is, hence, a misnomer. The use of the term 'woman entrepreneurship', however, holds significance contextually to meet the purpose of identifying women entrepreneurs who have only recently taken to manufacturing as their career overthrowing their traditional bondage to household activities within the confines of the four walls of house. Affective neutrality, non-conformity, perseverance, risk-taking and decision-making abilities, acquisitive-ness and leadership are the personality traits that an entrepreneur must have, irrespective of sexual identity. These characteristics have been culturally associated with men and there has been a conscious denial to women a work traditionally treated as demanding these personality traits in the person who carries it out. The trajectory of modernization and the new social order drawing closer has effectuated a new outlook to which women in the country have very positively responded and occupational modernization among them is an example of it. But this development is only at snail's pace.

Not many studies have been conducted on woman entrepreneurship so far. But, the studies carried out (Vinzey, 1987; Iyer, 1991; Singh, 1992; Sarngadharan and Beegam, 1995; Singh, 2001) have observed that many women entrepreneurs are either absentee entrepreneurs or for namesake. A considerable number of dropouts are there among them. They face the problem of role conflict and overburdening of multiple roles as men continue to expect them to play the roles traditionally fixed for them. They have a low self-image. A woman entrepreneur cannot spend as much time at the site of the enterprise as a male entrepreneur does because she has to look after household responsibilities too. Women entrepreneurs are generally hailed from families of smaller size and also have fewer children. Single women have been found to be more successful entrepreneurs. These facts suggest that the culture of gender discrimination has inhibited women's entrepreneurial ability and acumen.

Development and Displacement of Tradition

Traditional values are generally viewed as responsible for underdevelopment. Most people in traditional societies are not rational in their economic actions. Saving, investment, profit and acquisitiveness are not the concepts for them. They are dogma-bound and fatalist in attitude and are non-rational in their thinking and acting. A society which strives for development has to have a majority of its population being educated and modern, progressive and enterprising. They must be rational and innovative. A traditional society lacks such traits. The problem with most less developed countries is that they are not yet sufficiently modernized. They seriously lack in education, communication and infrastructure. Most people in traditional societies are conformists. They hesitate to adopt and innovate new things. People in such societies are assigned statuses by birth and, therefore, most of them do not strive to achieve position, status and fortune.

If it is accepted that the tradition inhibits or does not promote development, this also will have to be accepted that the process of development causes displacement of tradition. We have already discussed in the beginning that development and modernization have many common characteristics and therefore sometimes used interchangeably. We have also found that under the influence of modernization and development many traditional institutions have undergone drastic change in our country. Some instances of displacement of traditions as a result of development and modernization are discussed below:

Displacement of Traditional Joint Family

Under the influence of modernization and development, the traditional pattern of joint family is getting replaced by one or the other kind of household, which do not conform to the old joint family norms. Four fundamental characteristics of the traditional joint family system, viz., authoritarianism, low status of women, common property, hearth and roof and a large size have been challenged by the new social and economic conditions of the country. It is no longer so authoritarian and every individual, including a woman, now enjoy more or less considerable autonomy. However, it should not mean that nuclear family system is replacing the joint family system. Due to advancement in development processes and urbanization in India, quite a large number of nuclear type of small families are found to exist but such households are only a phase in the cyclical process of change in the family from nuclear to joint and vice versa. The nuclear family system is not in the psyche of Indians. Frantic migration and emergence of variety of jobs have led to the emergence of many types of family patterns. In essence, the joint family system continues to exist in the country.

Displacement of Traditional Status of Women

Very low status of women was a tradition of Indian culture. It was a potent characteristic of the patriarchal joint family system. As a result of the processes of modernization and development, we observe an improvement in their status. Women enjoy better status in their families now. They are on the path of empowerment. Education among them is spreading, their participation in gainful economic activities is increasing and they are achieving greater power to take independent decisions in their families. They are no longer confined to the four walls of their houses. This change from the very low status to better status is quite obvious but it does not present an egalitarian condition. Most women, despite education and economic independence, do not enjoy truly equal status in the family and society. Male chauvinism still continues. Even some educated parents discriminate against their daughters in their education, health and social activities. Even educated and working women are not enjoying autonomy vis-a-vis their husbands or other members in their families. In a study of women entrepreneurs, it was found that most of the entrepreneurs were only absentee entrepreneurs. The business units were only registered in their names whereas they were actually run by some man, which in most cases, were their husbands. Those who were looking after their business establishments themselves had to shoulder greater responsibility, work harder and longer and face greater difficulties. They had to suffer from work stress, multiple roles and conflicting roles.

Such findings alert social scientists to formulate precise methodological procedures for understanding the extent of women empowerment in terms of their autonomy. The extent of women's freedom from economic dependency and liberty to take significant decisions in family and personal matters needs to be matched with voluntary acceptance by their male counterparts. The level of compulsive agreement to their liberty may serve as a benchmark to measure the level of women empowerment.

Displacement of Traditional Social Structure

The social structure in India and elsewhere, before Renaissance and Industrial Revolution, had been more or less closed, highly stratified and ascriptive. The elite in such traditional societies defined social norms and wielded political power. The social system reflected the characteristics of strong familialism, particularism and ascriptivism. Thus, the traditional social structure represented the non-modern aspect of the binary opposition of pattern variables proposed by Parsons. These elements of traditional societies inhibit the process of development. On the other hand, the processes of modernization, urbanization and development also displace these traditional social values.

Displacement of Caste Structure

The caste structure in India has undergone a drastic change over the last two decades. The caste is no longer a way of life. Except for a very small section of old people with stubborn temperament, people in society need infallible institutional support to get rid of the hierarchical problems.

The pattern of interaction among people of different castes today is no longer strictly determined and governed by hierarchical order as it used to be in the traditional India. They interact on democratic principles in which everyone enjoys liberty and equal opportunity. The status of a person is not any more measured in terms of Dumont's model of purity and impurity of different castes.

Many castes in traditional India had their own occupational specialization, which continued through generations. People inherited the occupation of their own caste. They had no liberty to choose occupation for themselves. Instead, the caste chose occupation for the caste members. Occupational mobility was minimal. Some of these artisan castes were the barbers, the potters, the carpenters, the blacksmiths, the goldsmiths, the water carriers, the washermen etc. The processes of development as have taken place today have brought about drastic change in the traditional occupational norms. No longer is one bound to follow the family occupation. Occupational mobility, which was limited in traditional India, has now got accelerated faster and is all-pervasive.

Development and urbanization have not only generated occupational mobility but have also forced spatial mobility and status mobility. The spatial distance has made inter-caste marriages possible though endogamous marriage still prevails as a norm.

Untouchability was the most inhuman and detestable characteristic of the caste system. Spatial mobility, urbanization and spread of education have contributed a great deal to eradicate the problem of untouchability. The Constitution of India made the practice of untouchability as a cognizable offence. Today, untouchability in its original form does not exist. However, it cannot be claimed that it is completely gone. Untouchability, as an attitudinal behaviour, may not be expected to go for ever'. It has to continue in one form or the other. There is no society in the world where untouchability does not exist. Important to note is the fact that in the traditional Indian society untouchability existed at the corporate level to force a large section of society to have a permanent untouchable status. Untouchability today, if at all exists, is found only at individual level for purely personal reasons and not at corporate level for normative reasons. However, removal of untouchability, as it has happened in India is not so much due to constitutional provisions as to the processes of development and modernization.

We must emphasize here that all these changes are not absolute. They are in relative quantum. The traditional caste system did pose hindrances in the path of development in the Indian society. It inhibited the development of aptitude of acquisitiveness, innovation, risk-taking ability and occupational proclivity. The process of modernization, as it is taking place today, has made room for development in the country.

Development and modernization are mutually complementary processes. Both condition the evolution of each other. It needs to be emphasized here that the traditions of Indian society have not been completely displaced by modernization and urbanization, as has been the case in Europe. Milton Singer and Yogendra Singh are of the view that modernization has only trajectory inroads in the Indian social life pattern. Modern values have not replaced the traditional ones. Instead, Indian traditions have undergone modernization. The history of Indian social norms and values has been so deep and fathomless that it is just impossible for developmental processes to completely displace them.

Displacement of Rituals and Superstitions

Development is a process which takes place along the process of modernization, of which rationality is the fundamental characteristic. The ritual practices and observance of superstitions are fundamental characteristics of traditional societies. A society preoccupied by superstitions and ritual practices cannot allow an accelerated rate of development to take place. It does not mean that in the developed and modern societies religion is absent. Developed societies have no less religious-minded people. But, a conspicuous religious change, under the influence of social, political and economic modernization that is generally observed, is the radical reduction in family-level ritual practices and blind faith in all kinds of superstitions. It is largely because of the modern economic conditions, which have forced people to shun time-consuming ritual observance due to lesser time at their disposal. Non-rational belief in religion still prevails but religious practices are rationally decided. That is why, we find that not all the rituals and superstitions are disregarded; some rituals and superstitions are found as being observed by even most modern persons. Thus, the observance of rituals and superstitions depends on multiple circumstances ranging from basic needs to ambitions and achievements.

7 Technology and Development

Technology refers to the use of tools, machines, materials, techniques and sources of power to make work easier and more productive. While science is concerned with uderstanding how and why things happen, technology deals with making things happen.

Development is closely related with technology. The stage of development the human being has arrived could have been possible without the advancement in technology. The radical change and advancement in the economy, as we observe today, is the result of the modern technology. Technology has brought about efficiency and quality in the manufacturing sector. Technological advancement has reduced the risk involved in manufacturing enterprises. There has been tremendous improvement in the field of health the world over not only the average age of people has increased but the mortality rate has also declined considerably. This could be possible only because of technological advancement in health sector. There is perhaps no field of human life which has not been affected by technology. Agriculture, industry, profession, health, education, art, political processes, recreation, religious activities and daily life activities all are under the influence of technology.

But, it is important to keep in mind that technological advancement has affected human life both positively as well as negatively. Not only that life has become easy and comfortable, there are also indications of several threats to life and society in the future due to use/misuse of modern technology. The nature and extent of development the human society has experienced by now is heading towards crises in future. The sustainability of development is in question today. This has happened only due to irrational use of technology.

This chapter deals with the relationship between technology and development. It has been discussed here as to how development – economic as well as social – takes place with the advancement of technology but not without leaving a scar to threaten the human society. The development of technology, which itself is symptomatic of development, has brought about not only economic development but also radical changes in the social and cultural spheres of society. The chapter also points out the negative effects of technological advancements on social, cultural and economic aspects of human life. Technological advancement and development have come to a stage where human society finds itself at a crossroads. The positive as well as negative roles of technology have put humans into to a situation of flux and confusion.

Bright Side of the Technological Advancement

Technology is a broad concept, which refers to the tools that an individual uses for controlling, converting and appropriating environment, and for the sustenance of life. Human beings have been inventing technologies for making living possible and better. Human beings invented technology to produce and preserve fire that helped improvement in food and consumption pattern. Fire is one of the most indispensable resources on which human life depends. Wheel is another technology invented by human beings, which has made the mobility of people faster and farther. Communication technologies like telephony and internet have made every nook and corner of the world accessible in no time. Technology has reduced the time and space. Today, we can contact any person in the world by merely clicking a key on the personal computer.

Technology and Economic Development

From the collective economy of archaic society down to the present industrial one, technology has been an essential means of economic activities. The activities like production, distribution and management are carried out with the use of one or the other, simple or complex, kinds of technology. Technology is the means by which an economic action becomes possible.

Before the Industrial Revolution, the technology was rudimentary and human-driven. Only handlooms and handicrafts were in practice. The Industrial Revolution not only replaced the human power with machine power but also served as a gateway to a revolutionary development of technology and engineering along with the advancement of science. Since then, there has been successive development in the field of technology and engineering. The 20th century is marked by a passionate use of technology to appropriate maximum economic gains. Today, the use of technology can be seen in every field like agriculture, industry, education, transportation, communication and health.

Today, the economy has become global. More and more countries are participating in the global economic system. India too has joined the global economy. In the year 1991 the country introduced New Economic Policy with three major agenda: *liberalization, privatization and globalization*. It has opened its national boundaries for free movement of capital, knowledge and goods. By doing so India entered into a new economic regime.

Technological advancement has led to revolutionary progress in industrial development. The technology has improved the quality of manufactured goods, increased the efficiency of industrial production and tremendously diversified and multiplied industrial and occupational opportunities. Enormous growth has taken place in the service sector also in terms of emergence of unconventional jobs. The economy has become highly competitive in which people have been subjected to a work culture, which does not allow space for those who do not keep pace with the technological advancement.

Technological advancement has enhanced the quality of life and the standard of living of people. The radical developments in communication, transportation, entertainment and domestic conveniences have made human living quite smooth and comfortable.

Technology and Agriculture

Till the seventies of the last century, Indian agriculture was in a poor condition. The agrarian economy was largely consumption-oriented and there were poor irrigation facilities and simple agricultural implements. Agricultural yield was very low and dependency on nature was very high. The food grains were not enough to feed the population. With a view to augment the yield, the Indian government had no option but to introduce Green Revolution. The Green Revolution was a movement towards excessive mechanization of agriculture. The agriculturists were motivated and assisted to undertake the technology-based farming. Irrigation facilities were developed. Hybrid varieties of seeds were made available to the farmers. The conspicuous result of the Green Revolution was the augmentation of agricultural yield and a shift from pure consumption-oriented to modern market-oriented farming. Since then, there has not been any crisis of food grains in the country.

However, the results of Green Revolution were not uniform all over the country. Neither has there has been uniform impact on all kinds of crops nor has there been uniform impact on all the regions and all categories of farmers. The impact on other crops had not been as much as on the wheat. It is only the big farmers who gained much. Gujarat, Punjab and Haryana benefited more than other states. In Uttar Pradesh the western parts benefited more than the eastern ones.

Today, the agriculture has been highly mechanized. The process of harvesting, which used to be months' long involving a large number of people, has been reduced to a few days' work without engaging any major manpower.

The use of technology has reduced the risk factors in agriculture, particularly those unleashed by nature. Not only that quick processing has been made possible, technology has reduced farmer's dependency on, and vulnerability to, the nature. Even artificial rain has been made possible now to provide relief to the drought-hit villages. With the use of technology, it has also become possible to minimize the risks involved in agriculture to which the early farmers were awfully exposed.

The advancement in technology has introduced a new economy, sociability and consciousness among the people. The agriculture, with the help of technology, has got transformed into an entrepreneurial enterprise and is gradually taking a capitalist character. Some farmers have become capitalists in the sense that they make investments in their farms with fully calculated results to be achieved ultimately. Such farmers do not completely depend upon nature. They have their own means and methods to control the calamities unleashed by nature.

Genetically Modified Food

There have been radical bio-technological innovations in the field of agriculture. Through genetic engineering, the DNA is altered and a crop plant is created which may have desired traits such as resistance to pests and herbicides and increased yield. It is in 1994 that for the first time the GM tomato was commercially brought for sale in the market in the US for human and animal consumption. Such foods are produced from genetically modified organisms (GMOs). Genetically modified crops, it is claimed are, are (a) pest-resistant, (b) herbicide tolerant, (c) disease-resistant, (d) drought tolerant, (e) salinity tolerant, and (f) nutritious. So far, about forty plants have been treated by GMOs for commercial use.

Technology and Human Development Index

One of the important domains of development is social development. Modern values and innovative temper, humanitarianism and social justice, equality, liberty and individual autonomy and improvement – the Human Development Index (HDI) form the domain of social development. The people's health and hygiene, longevity and birth control, education and women's empowerment are also the significant indicators of social development. HDI, as formulated by the United Nations, consists of literacy rate, birth rate, death rate, infant mortality rate and maternal death rate. The advancement in science and technology has contributed significantly to the human development.

Technology and Health

Technological advancement in the field of health and hygiene has ensured healthier life to the human beings as well as animals. Generally, two things are important for better health and ensure medical treatment of a disease: one, diagnosis of the health problem and two, correct treatment of the disease. The present technological development has made possible the precise diagnosis of any ailment in the body making it easier for a doctor to administer correct treatment to the patient. There has been a revolutionary advancement in the field of surgery only because of the development of technology. From neurology to sarcoma no ailment now is incurable as was the view few decades earlier.

Earlier, there were high incidences of maternal deaths simply because of ignorance of the development of some kind of ailments in the body of a pregnant woman. There is now drastic reduction in the maternal death rate. Developing countries still have higher maternal death rates than the developed countries because the former do not have as advanced technology as the latter ones.

Certain women or men are biologically impaired to conceive and are unable to bear a child. The technology has made it possible for such couples to have children of their own through technology such as test tube baby or surrogacy. Likewise, the post-natal care of the infant was difficult and quite a good number of newly born used to die. But, now, the technology has made it easier to provide infallible protection to them.

Hygiene is a prerequisite for good health which can be ensured only with the help of technology at least at present where pollution of water and air is rampant and alerts the whole world. We now at domestic level use different water purifying technologies like aquaguard and reverse osmosis (RO) to make our drinking water palatable. It is the sophisticated technology with the use of which we are able to reduce the pollution of water, air and sound that we are now terribly vulnerable to.

Technology and Education

Technological advancement has also helped the proliferation of education. There is continuous research and development in introducing advanced technologies to make education easier, joyful and accessible. Education for children is no longer boring and cumbersome as the educational technologies have made it interesting. Studying by playing has been made possible only by the new technology. Distance education is now being offered by many universities and academic institutions to those who due to their personal problems are not able to receive formal education by attending the institutions. It is the technologies like TV and DVD, internet, telephony, which have made it possible to provide education to the recipient at a distant place. Indira Gandhi National Open University is a premier university offering distance education in India. Most Indian states have also established open universities.

There was a time, not long ago, when women were not allowed to receive education. A few women of the exceptionally distinguished families of higher castes did receive it but not in the educational institution outside home. But, generally, women were denied formal education. It is with the onset of modernization that people's attitudes, particularly that of the higher castes and classes, towards women education have changed. Though there has been tremendous improvement in the level of education among women, it is still far behind that of the men. It is not gender discrimination and male chauvinism which denied education to girls in the past but that the girls were not allowed to go outside homes for education for many reasons. They were susceptible to eve teasing and physical threats. Vulnerability was much greater when they moved around alone on the street. But, today, revolution in the field of automobiles has made it convenient for girls to go to educational institutions and coaching centres without much fear and vulnerability, no matter how far the institutions are. The number of female students has gone up today simply because of fast and safe conveyance apart from a shift in the attitudes of people from gender discrimination to gender equality. Thus, the role of technology in the expansion of education among women is enormous.

Technology and Empowerment of Women

There is a consensus among planners and academics that women empowerment can be assured only by guaranteeing two things: one, society's people, particularly women, must be educated, and two, women must be economically independent. Economic independence of women would not be possible so long as they do not participate in gainful economic activities outside home. Undertaking some kind of enterprise or taking up some job would be the only means to guarantee empowerment to women.

We have already studied in the preceding section as to how technology has helped impart education to women. We shall now look into how women's participation in the economic activities on a large scale would not have been possible without the help of technology. The traditional economy was simple, which required crude and unsophisticated technology and enough physical prowess. It is the technology of self-starter and computer, which has made women as competent as their male counterparts. Thus, the women have proved that they are courageous, hardworking, sincere and capable of doing any work quite efficiently, which is based on technology. Since they are physically not as strong as their male counterparts, they are obviously bound to lag behind them if the work is manual and involves hard physical labour. They might have not been able to drive bullock cart but their physical frailty may not come in the way of flying airplane.

Gender inequality has been a serious social evil the world over but is gradually fading out largely because of modernization, as a result of development in science and technology. But, male chauvinism still remains an area/issue to be tackled, which has shown little improvement.

Technology and Crime Control

It is true that crime rate may be controlled only when the state is sincere enough but it is also true that to controling crime depends on how precise the crime investigations are and how correctly the culprits are identified and punished. The advancements in forensic science have brought revolutionary changes in the crime investigations. With the help of advanced technology, it is now possible to investigate any kind of criminal problem. From lie detection test to DNA test, all those things are now possible, which were unthinkable a few decades earlier. Such technologies are aiding tremendously the administrative machinery in tracking down the nefarious and criminal acts.

Media and Society

There has been tremendous technological advancement in both print and electronic media due to which it occupies a vital place in the modern society. Information technology is the basis of the onset of the postmodern world. Today, it is the electronic media which defines the meaning of an object, generates and transforms values and creates image of every event and object. We know the world through media. The postmodernist scholars like Leotard and Habermas have explained extensively how the postmodern society is being governed by the electronic media.

Electronic media is now playing an immense role in maintaining law and order in society not only by revealing the clandestine criminal activities but also by awakening and sensitizing the public against probabilities of future crises. Judiciary and bureaucracy have also benefited much from the technological advancements in general and the electronic media in particular.

Dark Side of the Technology Advancement

Threat to Sustainable Development

We have earlier in this book discussed the problem of sustainable development at length. The increased efficiency of modern technology has led to faster exploitation of natural resources in the name of development causing serious depletion of renewable natural resources like vegetation and water. Earlier, the cutting/felling of trees was a difficult and time-consuming job. It was done manually by using axes. But, the introduction of advanced technology has made the task of cutting/felling trees much easier and faster resulting into startling reduction in the forest region. Global warming and depletion of ozone layer are the other adverse consequences of the excessive use of modern technology. We are aware that by 2050 almost half of the world population may be deprived of drinking water.

There has been also tremendous technological advancement in the field of agriculture. The farmers have now started producing genetically modified crops, which have both positive and negative impacts. It is, therefore, important that the technology should be used carefully and judicially. The dangers of modern technology are greater in the societies, which are not fully educated. It is, therefore, important that people should be made aware of the negative aspects of technology and make restrained use of it. Science has its own objective and course of action and technology will have its evolutionary growth. The need is only to be conscious about its rational application in the society.

Threats from Health-related Technologies

As stated earlier, the technological advancements have also made revolutionary improvements in the general health of people. Life expectancy level has increased and death rate has miraculously gone down. This has been possible because of the sophisticated technology being used for the diagnosis of diseases. But, the misuse of these technologies is also being noticed in the society now.

Imbalanced Sex Ratio

However, the sex ratio map of India gives disquieting results. The biological technologies are being used for unlawful and wrong purposes, such as the termination of female foetus. The alarming consequence of this nefarious activity is that in India, sex ratio is skewed in favour of males. For instance, according to the 2001 Census, the sex ratio in Haryana, Punjab, Uttar Pradesh, Delhi and Jammu & Kashmir was between 800 and 900, in Gujarat, Rajasthan, Maharashtra, Bihar, West Bengal and Assam it was between 901 and 950, in Chhattisgarh, Orissa, Andhra Pradesh, Karnataka, Tamil Nadu, Meghalaya, Himachal Pradesh and Uttarakhand it was between 951 and 1,000 and in Kerala it was more than 1,058. The data also reveal the fact that it is not only economic development which promotes modernization as is evident from the case of sex ratio and gender inequality in different states but more important perhaps is the social and educational development to achieve this end.

Surrogate Mother Technique and Threat to Kinship Norms

The modern technology has made it possible for a biologically-impaired woman to have her own child by borrowing the womb of another woman. The woman, who lends or gives on rent her womb to implant an embryo and relinquishes the child to be brought up by the couple whose embryo was implanted in her body, is called a surrogate mother. Thus, a couple that for biological reasons is not able to have a child may borrow a womb. Surrogacy is gaining the status of an industry of outsourcing pregnancy. In India, it is growing at a commercial level. In surrogacy, the embryo is transferred to the womb of the surrogate mother via in-vitro fertilization (IVF) method. There are places in the country today, which are known as hub of surrogate mother agencies and IVF clinics.

There are two major problems with this method. One, the professional lenders are generally the unknown persons. If they are habituated to alcoholism and drug addiction, it could have an adverse effect on the surrogate mother. The child thus carried in the womb of a sick woman with many bad habits may cast bad influence on the surrogate mothers. Two, the surrogate mother system poses a great threat to the family and kinship institutions in society. This will distort the norms and values of the family relationships and responsibilities among the members. This technology also poses an ethical question. Suppose, if the mother decides to lend her womb to her daughter, will not the relationship between the son-in-law and the mother-in-law be redefined? The place of daughter appears to be replaced by the mother. What will be the kinship relationship between the newly born and the grandmother, who played surrogate mother to the baby?

High Efficiency Weaponry and Threat to Life

Technology not only helps in controlling crime, but it also assists criminals in executing crimes more quickly, safely and effectively. Also alarming is the fact that highly sophisticated weaponry being used by criminals have capability to kill a large number of persons quickly. Today, the wars between nations might be more devastating as the countries, if left unchecked, may use biological and nuclear weapons.

Threat to common people had always been there due to the terror of burglars, dacoits, street snatchers, pick pockets and outlaws, but it was not as frightening and eye opening as is it today. Their onslaughts have now become much more terrifying only because of the increasing efficiency of the modern weapons. Terrorism, as it has expanded in the world today, though for multiple reasons, has acquired this scale essentially due to the mass killings and mass destructive technologies available to the outlaws. Sometimes, even the crime control department is not equipped with as sophisticated weapons as the criminals.

Threats from Agricultural Technologies

Though there have been remarkable achievements in the field of agriculture due to technological innovations, such as increase in yield, decrease in dependency on natural resources, safety from natural calamities like drought by creating artificial rain, agricultural hybridization and consequent variety productions and time saving in agricultural processing, the agriculture-related technologies have also unleashed negative impacts on people. The impacts would, however, be different in different societies. For example, high mechanization of agriculture in India, where a large number of people are engaged as farm labourers, would render labour jobless and they are bound to migrate to urban centres in search of livelihood. Besides, about 70 per cent of our population is still dependent on agriculture and the majority own such a small size of land that it is not feasible to use new technologies. This creates further economic inequality and class polarization.

Threats from Genetically Modified Food

Controversies emerged from the inception of GMF and the debate is still on focusing human and environmental safety. The advantages of the new technique are no doubt obvious but the apprehensions of dangers have not yet been confirmed. The dangers, which have been imagined by the scientists and common people are: (a) allergenicity, (b) environmental and ecological imbalance, and (c) and contamination of non-GM crops.

Due to the anticipated threats of the GMF, both the farmers and civil society groups have been protesting against its use. The civil society groups and the Indian government are at loggerheads over the issue, while the former want ban on its cultivation but the government appears to be reluctant to do so. The recent controversy over the brinjal in the country may also be seen in this context. BT cotton – another GM crop – has been allowed to be commercial cultivated but the civil society groups claim that would be dangerous for health and environment due to its toxic side-effects. The government is convinced to support the GM crops as they are pest-resistant and increase productivity.

Biotechnology and Threat to Human Society

The gravest negative impact of some of the modern technologies can also be seen on human society. New definitions, new norms and new relations are being created by the new technology. The relationship between individual and society and man and woman has been jeopardized by biotechnology. The principle of natural selection and environmental balance has been undermined by genetic engineering. If violent mice is produced, what would happen when cat and mice encounter? Is the pill for child control not tyrannical? What would be the picture of society when the designer baby is produced through genetic engineering? Horrifying is the very imagination of parents having all the freedom to have the baby of their choice. Society will have to control the choice of parents. The parents should not be allowed to go for designer babies like clothes in the market.

Science and Ethics

The whole discussion we had in the preceding paragraphs regarding the dangers of biotechnological researches raises the question of the limits of scientific innovations. As we have seen, there are both positive and negative roles of technology in the society. Some negative impacts involve ethical questions. The existing relationships between individual and society, man and woman and people and nature are threatened to be jeopardized because of some of the scientific inventions.

Francis Fukuyama wrote in 1992 his most popular book, *The End of History and the Last Man,* in which he opined that the western liberal democracy is the end of ideological evolution and the whole human society has to end with it. His thesis was incompatible with the thesis of Marx, and Derrida criticized Fukuyama for his interpretation of the end of history.

However, Fukuyama, later realizing that his thesis was not complete, wrote another book in 2002, *Our Posthuman Future: Consequences of Biotechnology Revolution,* in which he argued that the history will not come to an end unless there is end of the modern science and technology. In this book, Fukuyama warned us against potential threats of biological technologies to the liberal democracy.

Fukuyama's views are that biomedical advancement may possibly lead to alteration of humanity beyond recognition. In the history, from Plato to modern thinkers and dictators, there have been efforts to alter mankind for ideological ends. But, the current ability to manipulate the DNA of all or one person's descendants will have profound and potentially terrible consequences for our political order even if undertaken with best intentions. Fukuyama writes that 'factor X' makes us human. Moral choices, reason, language, sociability, sentience, emotions or consciousness or any other quality of human dignity come together to make up 'factor X'.

How to Resolve the Problem?

The modern technology has created havoc not only in nature but also has caused great confusion in the human society. The very natural man-woman relationship is being challenged by the biomedical sciences by artificial reproduction techniques. We have studied both the positive and negative consequences of technological advancements. We also know that it is not possible to curb the scientific explorations in a liberal democratic society. The only solution in this situation is the political will to regulate innovations and their application. This would call for a reasonable science policy to be formulated by the state and its ritual adoption be ensured. A law will have to be introduced to draw a line between what is acceptable and what is not. The parental liberty needs to be checked.

It is to be emphasized here that philosophy, theology or ideology may control science and technology within a limit and that too would require a terribly long period of time. What would really control the unrestrained and unreasonable use of modern technology are first the state and then the civil society.

8 Urbanization and Economic Development

Origin of Cities

City is a human settlement, a dominant characteristic of which is that unlike a little community, it is not self-sufficient. This is a basic characteristic of all kinds of cities – archaic or modern. Inhabitants of cities are not able to feed themselves entirely from the food produced within the bounds of the city area. In the context of old cities, this feature had greater significance as the cities were mostly walled and thus the term 'entirely' refers to the food produced only within the boundary of the city. Today, with a considerable degree of urbanization, the quality of self-sufficiency holds no significance as not even villages, what to say of cities, are really self-sufficient. As the economy advances, the degree of self-sufficiency is reduced and interdependence is increased.

The history of the origin of cities may be traced back to the Neolithic period when human population started moving from nomadic hunting life to settled pastoral and agrarian village life.

It is believed that in this age some small-size cities existed on the banks of the Mediterranean Sea in the south-west region of Europe. Kingsley Davis is of the view that cities must have originated around 6000 to 5000 BC due to surplus agricultural production required for trade. The earliest cities of Indian subcontinent, Harappa in Punjab and Mohenjodaro in Sind – existed in the Indus Valley around 2350 BC. These places, as claimed by archeologists, present enough evidence to prove that there was a quite developed urban way of life. Mesopotamia of Greece and Patliputra and Kashi in India are among the few very old cities of the world. Many historic and pre-historic cities, such as Mohenjodaro, Harappa, Nalanda, Taxila and Vijaynagar, are found today in the form of ruins. The other cities which survive today are Madurai, Patliputra, Kacheepuram, Varanasi, Delhi etc. The old cities were very small in size confining within walkable distance.

The Harappan civilization, which dates back to 2350 BC, continued till 1700 BC. The period after this is unknown as far as urbanization is concerned. It is from 600 BC that the evidences of the existence of towns and cities became apparent and two major civilizations – Aryan and Dravidian – came into being.

Urbanization, as we observe today, is closely linked with industrialization. Both the processes are complementary to each other. During the pre-industrial era, cities existed but their expansion by way of in-migration of rural population was not only minimal but also restrained. The concept of urbanization, therefore, does not apply much to the cities and their expansion, as they were, during that period. The cities, during the pre-industrial era, were broadly of three types: political cities, economic cities and cultural cities.

Political Cities

Political cities were the capitals of kingdoms. These cities were normally walled and inhabited by the state-related personnel, such as ministers and soldiers and persons with very special talents such as traders, singers, dancers, poets and intellectuals, jewellers and bankers etc. Entry into the city was not possible without prior the permission of the ruler, which could normally be granted only to extraordinarily talented persons. Henri Pirenne calls such political cities 'liege' type. Until the 14th century, such cities existed in Europe which, according to Pirenne, were mainly copmprised of priests and a number of artisans to assist them. B.F. Hoselitz writes that the 'liege' was a town of a community consisting of administrators, bureaucrats, teachers and students to which were added a number of artisans and servants for supplying them finished goods and services.

Economic Cities

As the name denotes, economic cities mainly performed economic functions. Pirenne calls them 'flemish' type of cities. These cities were commercial centres, where agricultural produce, artifacts, handicrafts material, non-agricultural articles and other finished consumer goods were traded. Such cities were mostly established on the banks of rivers, may be because of the fact that most of trade was carried out through the water route. Some of these old cities, due to their geo-political situation, could grow into big cities and others declined or disappeared.

Cultural Cities

The cultural cities came into existence mainly for their educational and religious significance. In India Patliputra, Kashi, Haridwar and Prayag are such cities. Most population in these cities was floating and, therefore, these could not be expanded much. The permanent settlers provided necessary services to the pilgrims and education seekers.

B.F. Hoselitz divides the post-industrial modern cities into two types: generative and parasitic. Though cities are responsible for both cultural change and economic development on one hand

and social disorganization and criminality on the other, the term 'generative' must be used in the context of economic development. The cities, which are characterized by a huge scale of heterogeneity, bring about cultural change and this, in turn, favours economic development. The cities which exert opposite impact are called parasitic ones. However, the orthogenetic cities do not necessarily impede economic development but lack of cultural change does discourage economic development. Robert Redfield and Milton Singer have opined that the primary urbanization is characterized by the development of 'great tradition' whereas development of heterogeneity, according to Hoselitz, may help economic development. At the primary stage of urbanization, there is always change in rural society. In the secondary stage of urbanization not only cultural heterogeneity takes place, but it also exerts unfavourable impact on economic development.

Urbanization

Urbanization is a process of change, which leads to the emergence and development of a human settlement with an ecological milieu and a style of life that marks a shift away from tribal and rural settlement and lifestyle. Social scientists take a view that it is a change towards civilization and development. The destination of this change, however, could not be confirmed indeed. The process of change in society has been evolutionary. The social scientists have used different conceptual typologies to explain this change. Change in society from simple to complex discussed by Herbert Spencer, from mechanical solidarity to organic solidarity by Emile Durkheim, from gemeinschaft to gesselschaft by F. Tonnies and from homogeneity to heterogeneity by Louis Wirth are the examples of typological interpretation of change in the sociological writings. This evolutionary change also refers to the change from rural to urban way of life. With the increase in population and population density in a specific geographical area, the characteristics of urban way of life evolve.

Urbanization can be understood in terms of the typology of city and country. Robert Redfield makes a distinction between what he calls a folk society and a non-folk society. The folk society, according to Redfield, has unlettered, homogenous and self-sufficient small population. This type of community does not exist. Redfield writes that no known society precisely corresponds to it. It was an ideal type of community, which was mentally constructed by Redfield for the heuristic purpose of explaining the process of change from rural to urban pattern of human settlement. The city, for him, is a place of people where non-folk type of culture exists.

Urbanization has a close link with the process of rural-urban migration. It is, therefore, broadly defined as a process of shift of rural population to what we call 'urban centre'. This process of people's drift to and congregation in a particular geographical space causes growth and expansion of the city. Urbanization is also a multi-dimensional process of socio-cultural change. It is, therefore difficult to give an all-encompassing and widely applicable definition of urbanization. It is because of its various aspects and dimensions that urbanization is studied in different disciplines of social sciences, such as geography, economics and sociology. On the basis of different aspects, urbanization can be divided into three conceptual categories, viz., demographic, economic and socio-cultural. The demographic aspect relates to the concentration of population in a particular area leading to the increase in its population density and in turn to the development of many other characteristics. The economic aspect refers to the movement of population from agricultural to non-agricultural sectors. This is a process of structural differentiation. Finally, the socio-cultural aspect is behavioural and relates to the change in the way of life. In the following paragraphs an attempt has been made to elaborate on these points.

Demographic Aspect of Urbanization

As stated above, the demographic concept of urbanization deals with the dynamics of population in a particular region. The demographic approach to understand urbanization has been used mainly by geographers and demographers. According to this approach, the process of urbanization and the growth of cities are the result of increase in population and population density. Urbanization, from demographic point of view, refers to the proportion of country's population living in urban areas. Increase in urban population of an area, over a period of time, is an indicator of the rate of urbanization in that area. The degree of urbanization is the percentage growth of urban population to total population of the country. If we look at the trend of urbanization in India since independence, we find that the urbanization during the period between 1961 and 1981 has been the fastest. Country's urban population was 17.3 per cent in 1951, which rose to 27.78 per cent in 2001. In 1961, it was 17.97 per cent, in 1981, 23.3 per cent, and in 1991, 25.7 per cent.

Urbanization and urban growth are two different, but interlinked concepts, but not necessarily complementary to each other. While urbanization refers to an increase in the percentage of urban population to total population, the urban growth denotes an increase in the total urban population. Sometimes, there is urban growth in a country without any urbanization. This happens when the urban population increases but the proportion of urban population declines. This situation arises when the growth rate of rural population is higher than that of urban population.

Rural-urban migration is central to the demographic perspective of urbanization. The urbanization, demographically, refers to the trend of shift of rural population to urban centres. The growth of urban population is determined by the natural increase in population, i.e., the birth-rate in urban areas on one hand and the rate of increase in urban population as a result of the influx of a section of people leaving rural areas, on the other. Generally, the natural increase in the population of cities is hardly higher than in rural areas. It is because the level of education, economic status and standard of living and accessibility to health resources, which are significant factors in the reduction of birth rate, are much more prominent in urban areas than in rural areas. Therefore, it is the shift of rural population to urban areas, which is largely responsible for the growth of urban population, is considered as the factor responsible for urbanization. B.J. Bogue and K.C. Zacharia, in their article "Urbanization in India" in Roy Turner's book *India's Urban Future*, have written that "rural-urban migration is by far the major component of urbanization and the chief mechanism by which all of the world's great urbanization trends have been accomplished." The discourses on urbanization in the academic world are mostly centred on rural-urban migration. Who migrates, where and why are the basic questions that evoke discussions. The classification of cities in India also has been made on the basis of the number of people living in different cities. Administratively, cities are classified into five categories on the basis of their population size:

Class I: one lakh or more population

Class II: 50,000 or more but less than a lakh

Class III: more than 20,000 but less than 50,000

Class IV: from 10,000 to 19,999

Class V: from 5,000 to 9,999

Economic Aspect of Urbanization

The economic aspect analyzes urbanization in reference to the economic structure of society. One of the major distinctions between rural and urban areas is that the rural economy is essentially agrarian, traditional and undeveloped, whereas the urban economy is, non-agrarian, modern and developed economy. Urbanization and economic development are coterminous and determine each other. The economy is divided into three industrial sectors, viz., primary, secondary and tertiary. Agrarian and land-based gainful economic activities form the primary sector, which is predominantly found in rural areas. The non-agrarian economic activities form the secondary and tertiary sectors in which the manufacturing and the service industries, respectively are included. The predominance of secondary and tertiary industrial sectors is a major characteristic of a city. The scholars are of the view that an urban centre is characterized by the fact that more than 75 per cent of the workforce of the city is engaged in non-agricultural, i.e., secondary and tertiary, sectors. It is because of this structural difference between rural and urban economies that urbanization is defined as a process of decline in the size of agricultural labour force in rural areas and proportional rise in the size of urban industrial labour force. The nature of the dynamics of this drift of labour force will be discussed at length later on.

Socio-cultural Aspect of Urbanization

Demographic and economic aspects of urbanization draw a boundary line around urban locale. Their efforts to analyze urbanization confine to the urban centre and to the elaboration of demographic and economic characteristics of the city. But sociological studies are confronted with much wider issues spread over much larger geographical regions even beyond the administrative boundary of the city, while analyzing the nature and extent of urbanization. Urbanization, according to sociologists, refers to the development of urbanism, which does not necessarily confine to what is called 'urban centre'. Urbanism is a way of life, which develops with the process of urbanization. It is the 'urban way of life' which is contrary to what is called 'rural way of life'. Urban characteristics are found even in rural settings to the extent they are developed and exposed to the urban centres. Urbanism, according to Louis Wirth, develops as a result of the growth in size and density of population. Urbanization is a process of evolutionary change, in a continuum, from rural to urban settlement and homogeneity to heterogeneity. Urbanization, thus, is a process of decreasing homogeneity and increasing heterogeneity in the community life of people. Thus, the sociological study of urbanization takes up, for analysis, the problems of social structures, i.e., family, caste and class, economic structure, lifestyle and values and norms, as undergoing change under the influence of urbanization. The concept of urbanism will be discussed in detail later in this chapter.

Urbanization and Modernization

Certain characteristics being common between urbanization and modernization make the distinction between the two processes blurred. It is because of this that these concepts often appear to be overlapping. The rationality, scientific temper, individualism, secularism, temperament of progress and mobility are the defining socio-cultural characteristics of both urbanization and modernization. Modernization refers to new cultural values, which emerged with Renaissance and Industrial Revolution and prevailed in European societies replacing the existing traditional social, cultural and political norms, e.g., feudalism was replaced with free democratic state, church was disjointed from state and secular nation-state was established, traditional agrarian and cottage and handicraft economy was replaced with industrial economy, customary laws were replaced with written legal system and people started becoming rational in their world view and individualistic in their relations breaking their subjugation to primordial authority of community.

Following industrial development the process of urbanization is accelerating at much faster rate. Urbanization brings about social and cultural changes in community life, which also correspond to modernization. The loss of group solidarity and community life and traditional large-sized joint families on one hand and growing individualism, and smaller sizes of households and development of autonomous personalities in a heterogeneous community on the other, are the commonly observed characteristics of urban as well as modern way of life. Cosmopolitanism, egalitarianism, humanism, secularism and democracy are the world views associated with what we call 'urban culture'. But, as stated earlier, this life is not confined to the population living in an urban centre. It can even be seen in the rural areas, which have greater exposure to the other dimensions of modernization, such as industrialization, education, communication and transportation. Sociology, therefore, conceptualizes urbanization in a much broader way, which would involve a more precise methodology with an exhaustive list of indicators of socio-cultural change characterized as urbanization.

Urbanism as a Way of Life

The socio-cultural interpretation of urbanization, as we studied in preceding paragraphs, clearly reveals that urbanization is a process of culture change under which the whole pattern of social life, values and attitudes of people get transformed into what Louis Wirth calls, "urban way of life" as opposed to what prevailed in village life. According to Wirth, with the increase in population and more importantly population density, the homogeneous nature of community undergoes change into a heterogeneous one.

Herbert Gens did not endorse the views of Wirth. He, in the year 1968, wrote an article, "Urbanism and Sub-urbanism as a Way of Life: A Re-evaluation of Definition" in which he opined that the Wirtheon theory of urbanism overemphasizes social dynamics of the central inner city and, therefore, it cannot be generalized to the whole urban area. In 'out city' quasi-primary relationship is found. Loss of kinship and primary community has been superseded by emergence of neighbourliness. Gens found that neighbourly ties are more intimate than professional and other secondary ties, but more guarded than primary ties of kinship and extended families.

Claude S. Fischer, writing on the theory of urbanism in 1984, endorses Wirth's size of density and heterogeneity and differs from the compositional approach of Oscar Lewis and Herbert Gens. Fischer emphasizes the fact that sub-cultures emerge due to increase in size and density of population. Thus, where Wirth's approach is ecological and deterministic, that of Gens is compositional and demographic and Fischer's theory is a sub-cultural one.

Rural-Urban Continuum

The urban way of life is an evolutionary process of change which has commenced from the earliest folk life. The finality of the urban life, however, has not been possible to construct as the future course of change is unforeseen. Louis Wirth, Robert Redfield and others, in conceptualizing 'rural-urban continuum', have identified certain characteristics to replace with those of the folk and rural societies. Redfield has conceptualized the first stage of human settlement, 'folk society' from where the process of change has begun. The 'folk society' was an ideal type constructed by Redfield only for heuristic purposes. No society exactly of this type, according to Redfield, existed. Talking of the characteristics of a folk society, Redfield writes: "Such a society is small, isolated, non-literate and homogenous with a strong sense of group solidarity. The ways of living are conventionalized into that coherent system which we call 'a culture'. Behaviour is traditional, spontaneous, uncritical and personal: there is no legislation or habit of experiment and reflection for intellectual ends. Kinship, its relationships and institutions are the type categories of experience and the familial group is the unit of action. The sacred prevails over the secular; the economy is one of status rather than of the market." As urbanization sets in, the characteristics that emerge are:

(a) growing population,
(b) increasing population density,
(c) increasing heterogeneity,
(d) declining community feelings,
(e) increasing formal and impersonal relations,
(f) increasing smaller household units,
(g) increasing individualism, and
(h) increasing non-conformist and mobility-oriented personalities.

Theories of Rural-Urban Migration

Lewis' Theory

The famous economist Arther Lewis formulated in 1954 a 'two-sector model' of rural-urban migration. There are two sectors: subsistence rural sector and modern urban industrial sector. The two-sector theory deals with the economics of labour transfer from subsistence rural sector to the urban industrial sector. Lewis' theory was reformulated in 1961 by Gustav Ranis and John Fei. The two-sector theory explains the process of transfer of labour from traditional low productivity sector to the modern high productivity industrial sector expanding due to increasing investment. Lewis is of the opinion that most traditional underdeveloped economies are essentially agrarian economies and have surplus labour available at a subsistence wage. The modern industrial sector is employment-generating and higher-wage sector. It is also characterized by capital accumulation and investment and consequent industrial expansion leading to increase in employment opportunities and existence of higher wages. These emerging conditions cause the transfer of labour from rural to urban sector.

Todaro's Theory

Todaro accepts the logistics of Lewis-Fei-Ranis model of rural-urban migration but only with reservations. According to him, this theory may correspond to the historical scenario of migration in the western socio-economic milieu but does not explain the trends of rural-urban migration in less developed countries.

The Lewis model assumes that there would be faster capital accumulation, which will be invested in modern industry causing new jobs in abundance. It implies that there would be labour transfer at the rate proportional to capital accumulation. But Lewis and his followers could not foresee that it could be possible only when technology would remain the same. But capital accumulation leads to capital-intensive industrial expansion based on advanced technologies, which yield high economic growth but there would be lesser labour absorption. The modern industry has limited labour absorption capacity.

Besides, Lewis' assertion that rural sector has surplus labour and urban areas have full employment, does not hold true necessarily. Urban areas in less developed countries in particular do not provide full employment. According to the Planning Commission, in 1978, India had 5 per cent of the labour force in the urban areas unemployed whereas it was less than one per cent in rural areas. Similarly, another report by M.S. Swaminathan Research Foundation (MSSRF) and World Food Programme (WFP) reveals that in 2002, unemployment was on the rise in urban India and current daily status unemployment is as high as 9.5 per cent for the lower expenditure classes.

Lastly, Todaro rejects Lewis-Fei-Ranis model for its assumption that there would exist constant real urban wages until the rural surplus labour exhausts. Todaro finds that in almost all less developed countries the urban wages have been on the rise.

Todaro's model does not advocate simply the rural-urban wage differentials as the basis of migration as is claimed in all migration theories. According to him, the migrant is much rational and calculative in his decision to shift to a particular city. He also takes into consideration not only the wage differentials but also the probability of getting a job in the urban area. Migration, thus, is determined more by rural-urban differences in expected earnings, rather than in actual earnings.

Following are the basic characteristics of Todaro model of rural-urban migration:

1. Migration is stimulated primarily by rational economic consideration.
2. Migration is decided on the basis of expected, rather than actual, urban-rural wage differentials.
3. Probability of obtaining urban job is inversely related to the urban unemployment rate.

Francis Cherunilam, commenting on Todaro's migration model, writes that while the model is correct in holding that there is no possibility of full employment in urban areas, it is not correct to assert that the act of migration is always rational and well-calculated. Todaro is also wrong in not giving any importance to non-economic factors in the migration process.

Lee's Theory

According to Everett S. Lee, there are four sets of factors, which influence the decision of people to migrate:

(i) Factors associated with the area of origin.
(ii) Factors associated with the area of destination.
(iii) Intervening factors.
(iv) Personal factors.

The decision to migrate is determined by two or three sets of factors in every area. While one set of factors motivates them to migrate, the other set forbids them to do so. Simultaneously, the intervening and personal factors also influence the decision.

Lee analyzes rural-urban migration in terms of push-pull factors. These factors push the rural population to urban areas and the urban areas have pull factors which attract them for inmigration. Broadly, there are five factors, which determine the push and pull conditions operating in the decision of people to migrate to urban centres:

(i) Economic factors
(ii) Demographic factors
(iii) Social and cultural factors
(iv) Geographical and physical factors
(v) Political and institutional factors

Economic Factors

The poor economic conditions and lack of employment opportunities in villages are the main push factors that drift the rural population to the urban areas. The rural areas, which are less developed, have poor agricultural conditions and greater population pressure on land, push the surplus population to urban centres. According to an ILO report, cited by N.V. Sovani in his book *Urbanization and Urban India* (1996), the main push factor causing the worker to leave agriculture is the lower level of income. In almost all countries, incomes in agriculture are lower than in other sectors of the economy.

On the contrary, better economic conditions, including employment opportunities available in urban areas, operate as pull factors to attract rural people towards them. Rates of migration to different cities are generally different depending upon the capacity of urban centres to absorb the incoming population and provide them sufficient livelihood. While some cities have greater industrialization and economic development, others do not have so much of development and employment opportunities. In India, cities like Mumbai, Delhi, Ahmadabad and Hyderabad had been pulling largest number of people from rural areas. Till 1980s the trend of migration had been towards such big cities. But, due to capacity saturation of such cities, the trend of migration has now detoured to the state capitals and other regional urban centres. Exodus of rural population to a few big urban centres of the country continues though not to the extent it was earlier. About 60 per cent of Indian urban population, therefore, lives in class I towns of the country. Frenetic migration of rural population to urban centres (particularly big urban centres), as we have been observing, has been due to the urban-centric industrial development policy of India. The economists, like Colin Clark and Lester Brown, have opined that the public sector expenditures in India and other less developed countries have been urban-biased.

The migration towards urban centres is not due to economic opportunities but also because of many other amenities and avenues. Educational and health services, higher wages, entertainments and better standard of living available in cities also pull the rural people towards them.

Since both the factors, push and pull, determine who, why, where and to what extent migrates, it is debatable whether push factors are more important or the pull factors. Most of scholars are of the view that rural-urban migration is largely due to poverty and lack of economic opportunities in villages are more significant factors than the availability of employment and other facilities. The push factors thus are more important to determine rural-urban migration. However, recent urban conditions have ceased to attract a large number of rural populations. Eminent Indian demographer, Ashis Bose is of the opinion that due to rising unemployment in urban areas, there is a trend of what he calls 'push back'.

Demographic Factors

Differential population growth rates in different areas determine the migration trend. Generally, there is higher fertility rate and natural population growth in rural areas. Due to better health services and educational proliferation, population growth in urban centres is relatively lower. These conditions are held responsible for rural-urban migration too.

Social and Cultural Factors

Social and cultural factors also play a great role in rural-urban migration. In rural areas, traditional values are much stronger and obligatory than in urban areas. Community is taken as superior to individual. On the contrary, in urban areas, the people enjoy much greater freedom and have liberty of unrestrained observance of modern values. The modern and western values are highly attractive to the youth. Therefore, this class of population is more motivated to urban-ward migration.

Today, there is acute shortage of agricultural labourers in many areas of the Indian countryside. Take the example of eastern Uttar Pradesh, where the main reason for this is the unwillingness on the part of the villagers to work on the fields of the landlords of their own villages. The traditional Indian caste-class structure has a great impact on the young population of the lower castes, particularly the scheduled castes. In the traditional rural economy, the scheduled caste people were destined to carry out agricultural labour work. With the proliferation of education, political development and radical arousal of consciousness among them, the young population among them now detests the higher landed castes and refuses to work on their fields. Only a few elderly people of the lower castes, due to their binding with the legacy of old relationships with zamindars, continue to work in the fields. The young population prefers to migrate to other places like Punjab or so even if they have to work on the agricultural fields. Working in their villages would not ensure as much the dignity as they now desire to be ensured in their lives. This situation has caused an acute shortage of agricultural labour in the villages forcing the erstwhile zamindars to sell the unmanageable parts of their land to the peasant class of the village. These kinds of developments have led to radical change in the class structure of the villages. The twin processes of bourgeoization and proletarianization have taken place to cause the swelling of the middle class of the villages, particularly of the north India. They spurn the erstwhile higher caste landlords who were the exploiters of their earlier generations and, therefore, migrated to distant places where they would work with dignity and decency. The older generation only, which had lived in the 'Mai-Baap' culture of the yesteryears, continues to work on the fields of the higher caste landlords and their youngsters are migrating to the urban centres. The cosmopolitan character of cities, with cultural diversities and individual autonomy very strongly determines the rural-urban migration.

Geographical and Physical Factors

Physical conditions, distances, climate and natural environment and natural calamities like tempests, floods, earthquakes and droughts have also been the determining factors in the nature of exodus of rural population to urban centres.

Political and Institutional Factors

The state policies regarding rural-urban and inter-state migration have played a crucial role in the transfer of population to the urban areas. If the state policy does not put restrictions on the free movement of population, the shift would be normal and exigent to the existing conditions. But if the state does not allow too much urban-ward migration and settlement in urban areas, the drift of population from rural to urban areas would be only limited. Mumbai has been a centre of great attraction for the Uttar Pradesh and Bihar poverty-stricken population but due to recent agitations waged by Shiv Sena/Maharashtra Navnirman Sena (MNS) have forced the inmigrants to go back to their native villages and also repelled the exodus of the new aspirants.

Urbanization and Development

Urbanization is a post-Industrial Revolution phenomenon. As discussed earlier, the urban centres of the pre-industrial era did not undergo any acceleration of urban growth as there were no pull factors in the cities to attract rural population. The Industrial Revolution brought about not only economic development but also an accelerated pace of urbanization, as the industrial development that took place in cities generated new and multiple occupations and jobs requiring a large workforce. The situation impelled the drift of rural workforce to urban centres keeping in mind the higher remuneration and better work conditions as compared to those in villages.

Role of Cities in Economic Development

Economic development is the direct result of technological advancements. The augmentation of growth and qualitative and cost-effective output – the prime objectives of a manufaturing enterprise – are possible only by the availability and proper use of efficient technology. Technological advancements become possible by researches and innovations carried out by scientists in laboratories. The scientific laboratories can be established only in urban centres as the infrastructural requirements of research centres may be fulfilled only there. The colleges and universities, the places of higher education and research, are and will possibly be established only in cities. The cities are, thus, the places of innovations and discoveries. Urban centres are characterized by high density of population due to which they facilitate much greater interaction among the people. As a result of physical proximity and consequent flow of informations, enrichment and diffusion of knowledge is made easier.

The technology, which is a precondition for economic development, is generally developed in cities. Even the advancements in agriculture are possible only in well-developed cities, as the agriculture-related technologies are produced only in cities and implemented in villages.

Trade is an important aspect of economy. A developed economy requires efficient and accessible commercial centres for the people to enter into commercial exchange. These centres are established in cities where necessary conditions and infra-structure for trade are available. Transportation, communication management and bureaucratic set-up, which help the trade centres work well, are established in cities only.

There is consensus among the scholars that the growth of cities is a necessary condition for economic development. Economic development requires greater degree of specialization of work and development of specialization is obviously possible at urban centres. Kolb's view is that industrialization requires universalistic achievement-oriented values to prevail and urban centres provide most suitable environment for such values to evolve. Likewise, Colin Clark is of the opinion that there is predominance of service sector industry in cities because of the fact that there is a high level of income. Growth of cities and rising income levels are correlated. B.F. Hoselitz says that the richer a country, the more urbanized it is and the larger a city in any country, the wealthier it is.

According to Robert Redfield and Milton Singer, primary urbanization is characterized by the development of a great tradition; and development of heterogeneity, according to Hoselitz, may help economic development. At the primary stage of urbanization, there is change in rural society. The secondary urbanization, Hoselitz says, is a stage in which though cultural heterogeneity takes place but exerts an unfavourable impact on economic development. At this stage, new techniques and technologies are introduced and commerce and trade normally increase. These conditions do increase economic growth within the city but this kind of growth is counterbalanced by depletion of natural resources.

Industrialization and Growth of Urban Centres

Industrialization plays an important role in urban growth. With the establishment of industrial units, the demand for industrial workers is generated and the workforce engaged in rural agricultural sector is transferred to the industries located in cities. Thus, greater the installation of industrial and manufacturing units, greater would be the shift of rural population to the cities, causing the swell of urban population and increase in population density.

Along with industrialization and urban growth develop many other subsidiary economic industries to attract rural people. Apart from multiple avenues of economic activities in the tertiary sector, such as the call centres, couriers, transportation, communication, care of children and the old and home delivery, advanced health facilities, good educational institutions, new and advanced entertainment avenues like multiplexes, gyms and night clubs etc. also develop in cities, which neither exist nor can exist in rural areas. These factors pull the rural population to urban centres. The theories of rural-urban migration, such as the two-sector model of A. Lewis and push-pull model of E. Lee, provide enough justification to the fact that industrialization contributes to the nature and extent of urbanization. Mumbai in Maharashtra, Ahmadabad in Gujarat, Bangalore in Karnataka, Hyderabad in Andhra Pradesh, Kolkata in West Bengal, Noida, Ghaziabad, Moradabad and Kanpur in Uttar Pradesh and lately Jaipur in Rajasthan are now among the most developed and highly urbanized cities of India essentially because of their faster industrialization and economic development. We also witness that many cities in the country Bhilai, Asansol, Tatanagar, Jamshedpur, Bhadohi etc. are known only for the industries established there.

Indian urbanization pattern has been lopsided. Class I cities, particularly the big ones, have grown faster whereas the smaller ones have stagnated. The regional and local cities have experienced zero to minimal inmigration. More than 60 per cent of the urban population resides in class I cities. The asymmetrical nature of urban growth in the country is largely because of the pro-urban industrial policies the Indian government has been adopting. It is only recently that the attention of policy makers has shifted from mega cities to regional ones and as a consequence, the trend of rural-urban migration has also shifted from cosmopolitan cities to regional ones like state capitals and district headquarters. The possible good result is the check on the frenzy shift of rural population to a few big cities like Delhi, Mumbai and Amritsar as has been observed till 1980s and regional cities have now started growing faster.

Urbanization and Entrepreneurship Development

Urban centres provide most conducive social space where entrepreneurship develops to a considerable extent. David McClelland claims that the child rearing practices, leading to development of entrepreneurial personality, are mostly found in urban families. Entrepreneurial personality consists of rationality, aggression, deviance, motivation for achievement, innovation and risk-taking ability. Such a personality is generally not born in rural environment.

Entrepreneurs are innovators. Such radical, deviant and non-conformist persons are generally not found in rural areas. Rural societies unleash pressure on its people to conform to the community norms and values. Urban people feel greater autonomy and do not find themselves under the pressure of community sanctions. Such conditions are necessary bases for entrepreneurial development. In India, entrepreneurship is largely an urban phenomenon. However, for the last two decades, the villagers, due to urbanization, infrastructural development and also lack of jobs, have been exhibiting entrepreneurial preparedness to some extent.

Urbanization and Rural Development

Development of rural societies needs, among others, infrastructures like electricity, energy, education, and a sufficiently good cultural environment. The Government of India launched 'Harit Kranti' sometime towards the end of 1960s. Stagnant agricultural production, which was pathetically low, could be augmented due to the introduction of technology in farming, irrigation and transportation. The agriculture is directly linked with industry and urban market. The agriculturist is now no longer dependent on nature. The farmers now may control the natural calamities causing damage to agriculture.

The means of mass communication, like television and radio, telephony and internet, have made it possible for the rural people to have access to global market. The agriculture in India is no longer of subsistence kind. The irrigation facilities and link roads to villages have contributed enormously to the rural development in the country.

Country-Town Nexus and Rural Development

Development follows a cultural change, which takes place as a result of spread of urbanism. Urbanism is a way of life consisting of a set of attitude for achievement and acquisitiveness, rational approach to life activities, sense of individualism and autonomy and rise of entrepreneurial spirit. The urban centres cast great impact on rural people leading to urbanization of rural areas. The world view and approach towards life also undergoes change.

Rural areas adjacent to metropolis and cosmopolitan cities have experienced faster change towards urbanization rather than those situated near small towns. If we compare the level of urbanization of India with European countries, we find that Indian cities are still not truly urbanized. Most of cities in the country have a mixed culture. Since rural characteristics are present in most towns, particularly the regional ones, there is hardly very conspicuous impact of urban centres on rural areas.

It is not because of the impact of cities but other developmental processes like education, modernization, transportation, telephony and internet that have really contributed to the urbanization of rural India. Besides, the latest trend towards the country-town nexus is also contributing in a big way to urbanization of rural areas. The city and its adjoining rural areas are developing a close symbiotic relationship. The town people are fed by the rural folk. They are supplied not only vegetables, grains, milk and other items of daily use by rural peasants and farmers but they also look towards the latter for labour and other services like those of domestic help, artisans and tertiary workers. On the other hand, the rural people receive money, market, employment, entertainment and modern culture. This give-and-take relationship is contributing to the development what urban sociologists have called 'rurbanization' a pre-urban stage of development.

Urbanization and economic development are interrelated processes. The nature of one is determined by the other. However, there are also many examples to confirm that these processes may also operate independently. If we look into the history of urbanization and industrial development in Europe, we find that both the processes started almost simultaneously. The pre-modern period provides evidences for the existence of urban centres without any role in economic development. The agrarian economy and urban centres existed unaffected by each other.

The linkage between urbanization and economic development is a conspicuous reality of the modern society that came into existence after the Industrial Revolution and Renaissance. Both the processes, as observed today, are complementary and also responsible for the development of each other.

9 Economic Reforms and Change

Indian Context

Indian economy will be remembered for its radical transformation from the year 1991 when the Central Government introduced the New Economic Policy (NEP) radically shifting away from the forty-year-long old economic regime of the mixed economy. This shift was not whimsical but a well-thought out programme corresponding to the experiences of the mixed economy India had been cherishing ever since independence. Actually, the experiences of the mixed economy had been very painful. Most of the public sector industries showed negative performances and some of which ended up either being sick or dying out. Many public sector undertakings also ran in losses. Lack of workmanship, guaranteed job, welfare programme and also lack of nationalistic sentiments in work made the public sector undertakings unproductive. The net achievement of the country after forty years of the welfare plight, with which the mixed economy was adopted, was its placement as one of the poorest countries of the world. The national reserve was empty.

Under these circumstances, the country had no option but to go in for a radical change in the old policy to salvage the nation. These situations forced the country to participate in the global economic system, which is clearly a capitalist one. India introduced the New Economic Policy in 1991, which incorporated three objectives – liberalization, privatization and globalization – when it was Prime Minister Narsimha Rao's government with Dr. Manmohan Singh as Finance Minister. This radical step was vehemently opposed by the major political parties in opposition but the imperativeness of this transformation was so positively realized that even the Bhartiya Janata Party (BJP), which opposed its introduction, when formed the government, reinforced it and termed it as the "second generation of the reforms".

Liberalization

Though the policy of trade liberalization was started in India on selective basis in the mid-1970s, but from July 1991 the policy of liberalization was taken up more radically and comprehensibly. The Indian government started relaxing control on trade leaving the exchange rate to be controlled by the market. Liberalization is an outward-looking policy as against the inward-looking one of the previous regime. The government allowed more and more individual investors to enter into any industrial sector. Most of the manufacturing sectors, which earlier were under state control, are now open for private investors. Delicensing is yet another aspect of the liberalization move. The entrepreneurs are no longer required to obtain permission of the government to establish an enterprise. The whole procedure has been liberalized to protect the manufacturer from the red tape. It has become now much easier for the entrepreneurs to establish manufacturing units without greasing the hands of bureaucrats and politicians as used to be earlier. The state also has facilitated the banking services for loans and other financial support to the entrepreneurs.

Liberalization has a significant role in promoting industrial development in the country, as the individual entrepreneurs are encouraged and the hassles emerging during manufacturing processes are minimized. Much greater areas are available for entrepreneurs to invest in as most of the manufacturing areas which were reserved for public sector have now been left open for private investments. The positive role of liberalization is exemplified by the fact that the number of small-scale industrial units of India swelled from one million in 1990 to about four million in less than two decades. This radical increase in the number of manufacturers is nothing but a result of the liberalization policy of the Indian government.

Since 1991, India started liberalizing its trade policy gradually and systematically. Restrictions on most of the items, except sensitive ones, have been reduced or removed. The quality control on import has also been liberalized. However, some restrictions have been increased as an anti-dumping measure. India is one of those countries of the world which has strict anti-dumping measures with reference to many items.

India has also liberalized its policy of Foreign Direct Investment (FDI). Except some sensitive sectors, FDI has been permitted largely in various industries. However, the country has been able to attract FDI to the tune of not more than 1 per cent of GDP. The disappointing records of FDI are largely because of the policy and infrastructural constraints.

Liberalization has benefited not only manufacturers but also consumers, workers, professionals and students. Liberalization of international trade has made any commodity in the world accessible to the consumer in his/her home market. The government has also relaxed the migration laws making it easier for workers to take up job in any country. The professionals like engineers, doctors and managers have now greater freedom and incentives to work in any country and more and more students of India are also obtaining education in foreign countries.

Privatization

Public/Private may be understood both as ideological and political concepts. Paul Starr, in his article, "The Meaning of Privatization", has pointed out the basic difference between public and private. Ideologically, according to him, both the concepts overlap each other. It is difficult to make a clear distinction between the two. For example, the economists consider the marketplace as private but for sociologists it is a public place. Public sphere is conceived of as open and visible – the sphere of public life, public theatre, public marketplace and public sociability. Public is essentially that which applies to all the people. Privatization then is a withdrawal from any of these public spheres. It is a withdrawal of affective interests and involvement from the sphere of public sociability. Privatization is thus a swing from civic concern to the pursuit of self-interest.

Privatization is a political concept too. It is a process of transferring the ownership of business from the public sector to the private sector. The concept of privatization did not gain currency before the rise of conservative political party in Europe and America around the late 70s and early 80s of the last century. Privatization meant a deregulation by the state of individual investment. The control on business swings the state to the market situations.

There cannot be very precise affirmative or negative views on privatization. Indian economy, ever since the introduction of the privatization policy in 1991, has invited eloquent and impassioned debate. Some, particularly those having communist leanings, are of the view that even if government moves along privatization, it should not privatize the essential sectors like power, airways, oil and natural gas and education. Their sympathies are with the workers and, therefore, they do not want them prey to the private business.

It has been the opinion of a few, particularly the communists, that privatization is key to economic development. Privatization may not be ingeniously, blatantly and illogically introduced. Privatization of education, oil and natural gas, water resource and electricity, for example, would create chaos in the society due to monopolistic attitude of the individual market players.

Under the policy of privatization, Indian government has introduced disinvestment measures in order to gradually wrap up public sector enterprises. But, it has been the opinion of a section of people that the government must see to it that a profit-making industry is not done away with. Others are of the view that government should keep itself away from the business responsibility as it can be carried out by individual businessmen. The state has more important roles to perform such as welfare of its citizens, primary education, market regulation and law and order etc. However, both the contesting sections realize that primary education must be under the state control.

The proponents of privatization are of the view that, due to free competition, market players can render better services and provide varied and quality goods. A private sector economy is a market-controlled economy in which lower the prices, better the quality of the commodity, much greater production, quick delivery and more choices are ensured.

The current state of privatization, at which the world economy has arrived, does not provide opportunity to opt for any one of the two economic systems: public sector and private sector. Privatization is the natural trend of economic development the world over. But it has been realized that privatization, apart from its merits, also leads to some unacceptable results. Actually, privatization has not fared well in all sectors. Hence, there is need for controlled privatization. The 'Club of Rome' working as a watchdog had brought out in 1970 its first report on the 'limits to growth' with an objective to warn people against the dangers of the use of outdated technologies and excessive growth. The world was also cautioned against the probable ecological imbalance and depletion of renewable natural resources, technology and construction.

The ultimate question that raises is whether the state can afford to become absolutely indifferent and unconcerned about the investments being made by people, irrespective of the industrial sector and the magnitude of investment, and also the norms of the manufacturing concerns regarding prices, wages and welfare measures for workers. The last two decades of privatization move by the Indian government have provided enough evidence to stress upon the fact that perhaps no state can afford to be absolutely neutral to its citizens' investment plight. The state shall have to continue as a welfare state and the dignity of human beings will have to be protected and promoted. This may be done only by the state and no other agency or individual should be involved in it. The maintenance of dignity of human beings would require effective checks on marginalization, exclusion, inflation, economic concentration, inequality escalation, prostitution and destitution etc.

Positive or pragmatic intervention by the state with a view to protect the interests of scheduled castes, the minorities, women and other excluded groups of the society would always be an important responsibility to which perhaps no state can afford to close its eyes.

Globalization

Globalization is a global phenomenon and now a global issue to be debated. This is not be a new event or process but, people of the world had neither heard nor used it. It is from the eighties of the preceding century that this concept came into currency and attracted the attention of the world community.

Broadly speaking, globalization refers to the free flow of capital, labour, technology, commodity and knowledge across national boundaries. It is a process of interaction and integration among individuals and nations of the world for the purpose of economic growth. The process of globalization has been facilitated by the modern high-efficiency communication technology like telephony, computer and internet. This process in a way is an international relationship without too much cross-border formalities and objections.

Globalization may be a novel concept but the relationship of international trade existed particularly among Asian and European countries. China was one of the leading international traders. However, the magnitude of this cross-border business was small and selective. The present international trade relations have gained new impetus under the new policy and technological development. Since 1950, the value of world trade has increased twenty times. From the year 1997 to 1999, the flow of foreign investment nearly doubled from $ 468 billion to $ 827 billion. Comparing the globalization of the past with the present one, Thomas Friedman has said that today globalization is farther, faster, cheaper and deeper.

Globalization is a composite process. A series of developments such as radical advancement in science and technology of communication, free fabulous movement of finance, capital and commodities, accelerated social mobility and national and international migration and consequent swell of diaspora result into what we call globalization. Globalization is also accompanied by intensification of cultural interaction among diverse groups through media exposure and marketing of cultural products. This is a revolutionary process, which is irreversible and may not be understood unless perceived holistically as it is consequent upon economic, social and political systems equally and simultaneously. Anthony Giddens said that globalization is not merely economic, it refers to a set of changes in economic, social, cultural and political domains. Communication revolution, according to him, is the sole driving force behind globalization. It is since late 1960s when the first satellite system was launched, the communication system gained revolutionary impetus and the whole world was knit into a close communication network.

Following are the domino effects of globalization, which endow it with a composite character:

1. Globalization is a nation's economic, social, cultural and political interaction and coordination with other countries of the world.
2. It believes in the capitalist system of economic relationship.
3. It is a process of democratization and concretization of individual autonomy.
4. It undermines state's primacy in individual's welfare. However, state's role of protecting its citizens may not be completely ignored.
5. The market governs economy.
6. The civil society or the citizens more actively participate in the democratic processes to ensure that the rights and dignity of human beings is safeguarded.
7. Globalization weakens the nation and national boundaries are opened for free movement of capital, labour, technology, knowledge, and commodity.
8. It increases economic growth.
9. It improves the standard of living of people.
10. It increases the cultural knowledge of people.
11. It swells diasporas.
12. It has aroused identity consciousness among people, nations and cultural regions.
13. It has increased economic inequality.
14. Most influenced by globalization is the middle class.
15. It has increased international migration.
16. It has promoted tourism.

Although globalization has encompassed almost the whole earth in its ideology and most countries have decided to proceed on this path despite its being irreversible, this process is not welcomed by all the countries on an equal footing. While some countries resist it, others have accepted and celebrated it. There are sections of people in most countries who do not appreciate globalization. Their arguments are that this is the process of hegemonic influence of America on the economies and cultures of the world. Both the Marxists and the advocates of egalitarianism foresee eventual underdevelopment of the less developed countries. The world system theorists like Gunder Frank and I. Wallerstein exposed the dependency of developing countries in their relationship with the developed ones.

Quite often are heard contradictory views on the concept of globalization, since the process is so complex and multidimensional that it is not easy to explain it clearly. However, it normally refers to integration of economic, political and cultural systems across the globe and also a process of Americanization or dominance of USA on the world affairs for others. While for some, globalization is a force for economic growth, prosperity and democratic freedom, for others it is a force for environmental devastation and exploitation of the developing world.

The academics are divided into two opposing camps over globalization: globalization skeptics, and hyper-globalizers.

Globalization Skeptics

The skeptics argue that the side effects of globalization on the society are much greater than its positive effects. One of the greatest skeptics, Ralph Dahrendorf, foresees a threat to social cohesion due to increase in individualism and competition. People become greedy and sometimes dishonest. He has expressed fear that we are to enter into an 'authoritarian century' because there would be intense conflict between the upper and lower classes, which would not be resolved peacefully. According to him, only 10 per cent elite class will be benefited in the globalized economy.

Paul Hirst and Graham Thompson and Held and McGrew are the great skeptics of globalization. Held and McGrew in their book, *Globalization in Question* (2000), have criticized the hyper-globalizers declaring the concept of globalization a myth, which conceals the reality of international economy increasingly segmented into three regional blocs in which national governments remain very powerful.

Hyper-globalizers

The best examples of hyper-globalizers are Japanese business writer Kenichi Ohmae's books *Borderless World* and *The End of the Nation State*. Hyper-globalizers are of the opinion that globalization is real and everywhere. It brings about accelerated economic interdependence and intense competition, which leads to qualitative economic growth. According to them, with increasing globalization, the nation-states are drawing to a close. In about next thirty years, there would be 100, 200 or 300 city states replacing nation-states. Hong Kong, London, Frankfurt, Barcelona and Mumbai are in direct interaction with the world without linking themselves with the regional economy.

Anthony Giddens favours hyper-globalizers but argues that both hyper-globalizers and skeptics are mistaken. Globalization, according to him, is not merely economic. As stated earlier, it refers to a set of changes in economic, social, cultural and political spheres and, the sole driving force behind this change is the communication revolution. Alberto Martinelli of Italy also defines globalization as a set of processes, which interconnect individuals, groups, communities, states, markets, and corporations, international governmental and non-governmental organizations on the complex web of social relations.

National boundaries, as existed traditionally in the pre-globalization period, forbade integration at the international level. They create the psyche of discrimination and hatred towards trans-boundary people. Giddens gives the example of the Berlin Wall. Before the wall was dismantled, if someone crossed the boundary, he was ill-treated by the sentry. But ever since the wall has been removed, the psychology of the people of both sides has changed entirely and they love each other.

Globalization has got to have the same effect on people the world over. The national segmentations would be abridged and a global fraternity will be founded.

Favouring globalization, Giddens argues that this is a process of change, which promotes self-identity consciousness among people. The individual creates self-identity rather than taking it from cultural background. Globalization is a process which leads to individualization and growth of reflexive life looking for open future.

Let us now close the intellectual debate on the positive and negative aspects of globalization here and concentrate on its consequences on the Indian society and polity. Globalization is a free movement of everything across the country. This means that there would be free transfer of capital, labour, commodity, technology, knowledge, data, idea, diseases, pollutions and infections. Since globalization promotes an interpersonal relationship at the global level, it will have both positive and negative consequences.

India is the fastest growing economy today after China and it can be safely said that in about forty years from now it will be advanced so much so as to top the list of the developed countries. But, the present scenario does also cause an anxiety among the people of the country. India lags behind the neighbouring country China despite having similar historical and demographic conditions. By 2004, China had the foreign investment as much as 60.6 billion dollars whereas in India it has been only to the extent of 5.3 billion dollars. Both the countries have almost the same percentage of FDI to the GDP but that amounts to 50 billion dollars for China whereas for India it is only 4 billion dollars. Despite being a closed economy, if China attracts this amount of FDI, it deserves appreciation. However, there are studies to prove that China's information about the net FDI is not authentic as they include many such items that do not fall in the list of categories, which constitute the total of FDI amount, whereas India does not include certain items, which are approved by the IMF. Nirupam Bajpai and Nandita Dasgupta suggest that India should include certain items in the definition of FDI. However, despite definitional disagreements, we have no reason to deny the fact that, as stated by Bimal Jalan, former Governor of Reserve Bank of India, we are the least globalized among major countries of the world.

Alberto Matinelli provides definitional oppositions based on three axes: one, the axis of globalizers and skeptics where the key distinction concerns the degree of novelty of globalization and its impact of nation-states; two, the axis of neo-liberals vs neo-Marxists and radicals where the key points are the balance between the positive and negative impacts of globalization and its truly global western hegemonic character; and three, the axis of homogenization vs heterogeneity and hybridization which focuses upon cultural dimension of globalization.

Thus, views and definitions of globalization differ enormously in relation to the nature, aspects, causal dynamics, timings and trajectory actors, and social impact on people in terms of new patterns of hierarchy and inequality and political implications.

Types of Globalization

Economic and cultural are broadly the two types of globalization. These domains are also interconnected. Development of communication technology like telephony, television, computer and internet has been the only instrumental factor to bring about economic and cultural globalization. At the root of the globalization is technological revolution, which has squeezed time and space in bringing people of the world in contact with one another as and when one so desires. Its direct bearing is on the possibility of economic interdependence among the world countries.

Economic Globalization

From the second half of the eighties of the preceding century, a radical economic relationship among different countries has come into being which is governed and regulated by the market. The Indian market is now replete with both domestic and foreign manufactured goods. FDI is gradually increasing in the country and also the neighbouring countries. Multinational companies are joining hands with Indian companies in a big way. However, economic globalization in India is still scanty and partial and needs to be evaluated with reference to the other countries of Asia, particularly China. Globalization is an economic change, which is characterized by increasing consumerism and a non-conventional and trendy lifestyle. The consumption pattern, cultural production and other local cultural categories undergo change away from the traditional living pattern. The markets are flooded with a variety of goods manufactured all over the world. India has joined the globalization movement and has indeed left an imprint on the world economic system by contributing enormously, particularly in the knowledge industry sector. The country is proud of the fact that the developed countries are now forced to look towards India for the new challenges that have emanated from the development.

Under the process of globalization, there is free movement of capital and commodities from one country to other. The businessmen of one country are freely investing money in manufacturing, service, knowledge and other sectors of other countries. Multinational companies are mushrooming and dominating the indigenous manufacturing sector of the less developed countries.

Cultural Globalization

Globalization of cultural items is a natural outcome of economic interdependence and reciprocal relationships. Efficiency of communication technology and consequent economic linkages determine the extent and nature of cultural symbiosis among the involved countries. Cultural expansion across national boundaries is a natural result of intense economic globalization. Mass media has an important role to play in bringing the cultures of the world to people anywhere in the world, who adopt them if influenced. Since the education and urbanization have weakened the old institutions and community cohesiveness, and strengthened individual autonomy, the process of imitating foreign culture has been accelerated.

Cultural globalization takes place at two levels. One, every culture of the world is exposed to the people of every country through mass media and thus all the local cultures are interacting with one another. In this process of cultural symbiosis, all the cultures are taking global character in varying degrees depending upon their attractiveness to people outside their cultural boundaries. Cultural globalization is quite visible today in the form of uniformity of dress style, consumption pattern, food habits etc. People, particularly the youth, are frantically following the new lifestyle. The mass media has brought people closer to the cultures of the world, which were earlier completely unknown to the people at distant places. The television channels on geography, tourism and wildlife have contributed a lot to culturally unite people of the world ignoring specificities. Professor Yogendra Singh says that globalization has also changed the traditional mode of cultural expressions, usages of language and communication media at the local, regional and national levels. These have also created many sub-cultures of entirely new kind in urban areas. The rise of popular culture is a new phenomenon with linkages both to rural and urban areas.

At the other level, globalization has accrued the material benefits to the local cultures. The local cultures of India, which were confined to local spaces and carried out either as part of leisure by local artisans or could be decoration pieces and items of pleasure for the local elite, are now expanding much beyond their traditional boundaries. These culture products were not the commodity of the market. The artisans of these arts and artifacts were doomed to live a modicum of life. As a result of globalization, the local cultures are getting commoditized and monetized and enjoying their existence at global level, making handsome amount of money for their creators, the craftsmen, ameliorating their destitute and raising the standard of living.

One thing, however, has to be borne in mind that, under the influence of globalization, market economy, media, efficient and powerful information technology and the local cultures are forced to undergo some changes and some degree of homogenization of culture, which is not difficult to notice. But this does not mean that the local cultures will vanish completely and there would be one culture pattern the world over. A large amount of self-identity and autonomy is enjoyed by local cultures. This is also truer about the Indian local culture. In reality, the greater the depth of history of a culture is, greater would be the resistance to the external pressure to it as is the case with Indian culture. M.N. Srinivas writes:

> Indian culture is characterized by enormous diversity. It would not be an exaggeration to say that the cultural situation in India varies every few miles. And even within a single village, each caste has culture which is somewhat different from that of the other. In fact, it would not be an exaggeration to state that each kinship unit has its own distinctive cultural practices, representing a fusion of different incoming affine strands modifying the culture of the main agnatic stem.

It is because of this strength that the local cultures of India have enough resilience to counter hegemonic impact of globalization on them. India is a very successful democracy. The state takes care of the interests of people of the country and does not allow the negative consequences of globalization to prevail but if the state fails at some point people enjoy so much autonomy and power that they resist the negative influence of globalization by resorting to democratic means like demonstrations, strikes, street plays and many other methods, which are even violent sometimes. Civil society is gaining power and confidence to counter the wrongs of globalization. Today, no international deal undertaken by the government goes unattended by the people of the country. For example, the recent Indo-US nuclear deal, which was ratified not only after an intense debate but also led to a confidence motion for the government and then only it got the nod of the country.

Globalization and Local Identity

We have mentioned earlier that globalization is not a new phenomenon. Trade relations between Indian and foreign people existed even in the olden days. International migrations also had been there in those times. There is no reason not to believe that economic and corresponding cultural globalization were present at least during the medieval period. This process gained a little acceleration during the British times. The modern industry was introduced in India by the British. M.N. Srinivas writes that the westernization was a process of culture change that took place in India as a result of the presence of the British in the country for a pretty long period of time. Thus, economic relationships and cultural symbiotic contacts existed even before the dawn of globalization as we have come to understand this process now. The only thing which has attracted our attention is the fact that the momentum of globalization process is highly accelerated and the space covered by it is much wider.

As the time and space have got squeezed under globalization due to revolutionary advancements in information technology and the lifestyle of people, particularly the youth, has undergone drastic change, a natural trepidation among people has been that globalization would lead to cultural homogenization, loss of statehood and lack of identity – local, regional and national. But soon this consternation proved to be baseless as despite radical changes in lifestyle – dress, food, work and leisure – local identity is not being overshadowed absolutely, rather it is getting reinforced in many respects. The fact that is emerging today is the coexistence of both global as well as local cultures. Thus, a new process of glocalization, which we will discuss later, is taking place. Glocalization is a process of globalization, which, instead of replacing local culture, adapts to it and incorporates it to arrive at mutual adjustment and not a confrontation against each other. The culture thus emerged is a culture which consists of elements of both foreign and indigenous cultures. Indian situation is still more complex to understand in relation to globalization as the country is one of the major players in the process of globalization and maintains its strong cultural identification as well.

Indian Situation

India is a country of cultural diversity. It is cultural pluralism, which characterizes the success of a democracy. Indian society consists of caste-based, religion-based and tribe-based plurality of communities representing continuity and historical linkages. There has been interaction between local and regional cultures and the fluid nature of culture allowed inter-cultural reciprocity. Sociologists have noticed that through centuries, there have been the processes of 'universalization' and 'parochialization' of regional and local cultures, respectively. There has been a continuous dialogue and even creative synthesis between the 'great tradition' or elite culture and the 'little tradition' or the folk or local culture. However, the local identity of culture never vanished.

The 'Peoples of India' report of the Anthropological Survey of India, published in 1992, is a true testimony to the existence of cultural plurality and continuity of cultural identity in the country. According to the report, 4,635 communities have been identified in the country. These communities have been defined at the various levels through which they identify themselves: castes and sub-castes, minorities, linguistic and cultural categories. The report has its own definitions of communities to locate the categories with special ethnic characteristics ranging from castes and minorities to those who identify themselves through cultural categories, including language (such as Assamese, Bengali, Gujarati, Rajasthani, Tamil etc.). Of the total 4,635 communities, 796 are distributed over the larger part of the country. More than one hundred communities perceive their dispersal internationally, and most of them interestingly come from the states of Mizoram, Meghalalya, Sikkim and Tripura.

The communities have their own local and regional cultural identities, which are reflected through normative patterns and style of life, such as social and cultural practices, design of the dress including turban, community flags and ornaments and the ornamental decoration of the body. The report concludes that in spite of conflicts and contradictions, we find continuity and a sense of harmony existing over a large part of the country. It is interesting to note that the issue of localism and nativeness has become a less sensitive matter as very few communities are there in India which consider themselves to be migrants. This is commonly expressed through their folklores and folktales. Thus, India may also be called a land of migrants.

Cultural Identity

Cultural identity is a historical reality. It evolves through history in the form of living patterns and beliefs and practices. Yogendra Singh writes that cultural identities are shaped by a complex set of factors, which are associated with the processes of evolution of cultural practices and beliefs of a people in course of their historical experiences. Ecological setting, basic economic institutions and work related to it, the family structure and child rearing practices, stories, legends and myths along with history, constitute some of the elements which give identity to a culture as it manifests itself through symbolic expressions in material artifacts, expressive behaviour, belief systems, language, literature, etc.

This is a common fear that the local culture and its identity would be wiped out under the camouflage of the globalized culture or the culture of the developed capitalist countries. But, contrary to this, there is no evidence of any threat to the basic cultural identity of a person or a community as a consequence of globalization. The local cultures are not only surviving the onslaughts of global culture, if any, but also gaining broader premises expanding sometimes upto the transnational regions and becoming more meaningful in the modern market context.

There is no major threat to local culture for the following reasons:

(a) The culture (behaviour pattern, language, belief system, norms and values etc.) is internalized by human beings and thus forms the basic personality structure, which resists major adoption of any outside culture. A part of it, however, is accepted by rationalizing through new ideology. Most cultural changes take place only in peripheral cultural premises. The core culture hardly allows a radical change in its fabric. However, cultural identities constitute a dynamic process corresponding to socio-economic and techno-ecological changes encountered by the community.

(b) Globalization is not an all-pervasive process to embrace each and every section of the society in its ambit. Mostly, the middle class and particularly the youth are exposed and susceptible to the impact of globalization. This is hardly 35 per cent of the Indian population.

(c) Globalization is an intermixture of multiple cultures and not replacement of one culture by the other. There is co-existence and reciprocity of both global and local cultures.

(d) Globalization has reduced the gamut of institutional power of the nation. Gradually, it is shirking from its welfare-related responsibilities. The most important role the nation continues to perform is the international trade rules regarding items of basic needs and strategic importance. In the event of erosion of significance of the nation, the civil society formation is gaining impetus and a citizen is becoming more and more identity conscious and resisting any threat to local culture. The Indian diasporas are the best examples who have started living their indigenous cultural lives with much greater fervour and vehemence than before. The greater the threat from outside, the more intense would the cohesive and integrative processes in a community be.

(e) Globalization is indeed an irreversible process. It is more natural and evolutionary than intended and designed. But it is least all-encompassing due to the two realities existent at two levels: one, the globalization process and the impact exerted by it are not uniform the world over; and two, all cultural patterns and their history and seriousness are not uniform the world over to receive the impact uniformly.

Glocalization

Glocalization is a term which combines the processes of globalization and localization. This term was first used by Japanese economists in late 1980s. It was referred to as an effort to make the products adaptive to the specific culture they are to be marketed in. Glocalization thus negated the threat of extinction of local culture as the market now attempts to be local culture-friendly. Globalization, in order to promote products, attempts to adjust to local cultures. The term 'glocalization' was popularized by Ronald Robertson, who noticed the assertion of local culture at global level. In a seminar on 'Globalization and Indigenous Culture' he observed that glocalization means simultaneity and co-presence of both the processes of universalizing and particularizing tendencies.

McDonalds, a chain of food courts, which has its presence the world over, presents a peculiar example of globalization. In order to capture the market in every nook and corner of the world, it attempts to prepare their staff to make the food palatable to the local culture. The best example of globalization is the fact that in order to promote the marketing of its products in France, McDonalds changed their conventional mascot to asterix – the gaul – a popular French cartoon character. McDonalds would not mind serving Dosa (a South Indian dish) to their customers if they are established in a city of southern India where it is a common food. Choorma-Bati of Rajasthan and Bati-Chokha of Bihar may one day become servings of McDonalds if established in respective states. These happenings do negate any possibility of threat to local identity of a culture.

We presume that global marketing system may bring about a coalition of different cultures but individual identity would not be compromised and people will always try to keep themselves distinguished from others which would require sustenance of distinguished features of local culture. Thus, the mix-up of market economy and local culture is a non-issue.

Globalization and Popular Culture

The popular culture is the culture of masses manifested through their cultural practices. It is a pattern of human activities and their symbolic expressions, which are popular and widespread among people. Historically, the difference existed between the culture of elite and the culture of masses. The globalization has brought about tremendous changes in the cultural patterns by bringing both elite and mass cultures together. The differences between the elite culture and the local culture have been minimized to a negligible number.

With the change of traditional feudal economy into capitalist market-oriented one, a new form of cultural differentiation has taken place. The social structure no longer determines the cultural style. The cultural patterns along caste hierarchy and the cultures of the elite and peasant workers have undergone new differentiation. The new culture forms that have emerged are described as 'popular culture' or 'mass culture'. Popular culture is the result of technological advancements in mass media and communication. Unlike folk-elite culture forms, it is not based on communitarian social structure governed by tradition. Popular culture is produced and governed by free-floating market forces.

Folktales, folklores and mythological stories are the sources of popular culture and they comprise human activities in every walk of life, such as eating, drinking, dancing, singing, playing, child rearing, merry making, work and leisure, entertainment, etc. The wide spectrum of human behaviour patterns of the common masses, which are projected through mass media, forms the popular culture.

Globalization is the post-modern economic process in which the distinction between the so-called low and high cultures is blurred with the rise of local culture at national and international levels and the diminishing effect of hegemonic culture of the elite. Rising popularity of the culture of the masses has thwarted efforts to eliminate or replace local culture. Under the influence of capitalist economy, the less developed countries have, instead, gained advantage of enriching their popular cultures by popularizing them at international levels and also commercializing them in the global market thus bringing the artisans and artists out of the modicum of living they had been destined to for centuries.

Yogendra Singh, in his book *Culture Change in India,* has observed that the growth of popular culture coincides with deeper social transformation in society. The indicators of this change are: disenchantment with the traditional rural life, massive migration to cities, growing charm of consumerism, tremendous expansion of psychic and social mobility of people with corresponding weakening of the bonds within family kin group and local communities. Popular culture also coincides with the rise of individualism and individual's search for perpetual renewal of experiences.

Ever since the onset of globalization, there has been a fear psychosis in the minds of people, particularly of the developing countries, that cultural hegemony of the West and consequent eclipse of the local cultures is inevitable. But neither it happened over the last twenty years of the emergence of the process of globalization nor is there any threat of this kind as cultures do not get extinguished but only undergo change and manage to co-exist. People are found accommodating well with the contrasting cultures. It is found that people are observing family norms and values and also simultaneously enjoying the McDonalds and Barista cultures.

People in villages have enjoyed traditional cultural autonomy and continue to do so despite their being sufficiently urbanized and modernized. Thus, cultural hegemony and eclipse of local culture is only a myth. The culture would instead be enriched by interaction among different cultures of the world. The process of globalization thus is not disintegrative but only integrative.

10 Modernization

Social change has been the most crucial subject matter of study in sociology right from the origins of the discipline. It would not be inappropriate to say that sociology emerged in order to understand the process of change in society. All the early sociologists have, therefore, propounded almost similar type of dichotomous characteristics to explain the evolutionary direction of change of societies. Emile Durkheim's mechanical solidarity vs organic solidarity, Ferdinand Tonnies' gemeinschaft vs gesellschaft, Pitirim Sorokin's military society vs industrial society and Herbert Spencer's undifferentiated homogeneity to differentiated heterogeneity are some of the exemplary polarities in classical sociology, which explain the pattern of change. All these views have one thing in common and, that is, the pattern of change is evolutionary. The dichotomy of tradition vs modernity is a belatedly created conceptual schema, which is consistent with the above dichotomous conceptualizations and represents the continuum of change in society from traditional world view to modern world view.

The concept of modernization is a post-Second World War formulation when the Asian, African and Latin American countries became free from the colonial rules and moved on the path of development. These countries formed a political region, known as the 'Third World'. The western scholars started to study the social change as taking place in these post-colonial societies with a comparative perspective by using the West as a reference model. The society, polity and economy of the West, as it developed towards the close of the 18th century in response to Industrial Revolution and Renaissance, came to be considered as modern and those of the Third World as traditional. Modernization, thus, came to be defined as the changes taking place in the social structure, cultural world view and the economic system in the less developed countries as a result of the influence of western societies. To put it differently, the changes in developing countries, taking place on the pattern of the West during the latter half of the 18th century, came to be termed as modernization. The polar types of concepts like gemeinschaft and gesellschaft or mechanical and organic solidarities were used to explain the patterns of change in culture, polity and economy of European societies and that of tradition and modernity in Asian and African societies. However, Yogendra Singh, writing on modernization of Indian traditions, emphasized that, for historical reasons, not all changes may be called modernization. The basic direction of change in India, due to western contact, was towards modernization but in the process a variety of traditional institutions also got reinforced.

We have already discussed in the preceding chapters that modernization and development have many common characteristics due to which both overlap each other and are sometimes used interchangeably. However, the concepts have their separate analytical and heuristic significance. The lack of distinctiveness is natural because the processes started simultaneously and determined each other's progress.

Defining Modernization

Daniel Lerner was one of the earliest scholars to have studied modernization and discussed his views in his book *The Passing of Traditional Society*. According to him, modernization is a global process with rationalist and positivist spirit. The process would result from urbanization and proliferation of literacy and consequent expansion of mass media. Modernity comes through change not only in institutions but also in persons. A person, who is modernizing himself, according to David McClelland, needs to develop strong desire to do something better (achievement motivation). Almost all the early scholars, who associated themselves with the modernization theory, commonly believed that modernization is an evolutionary process.

Talcott Parsons may be considered to be the first scholar to have propounded a systematic theory of modernization. He suggests that for societies to move from the primitive to the modern, several 'evolutionary universals' have to be present. Evolutionary universals, according to Parsons, refers to any complex of structures and processes, which increases the adaptive capacity of the systems. Three pattern-variables are important indicators of a society moving on the path of modernization:

1. achieved status in place of ascribed one,
2. universalistic norms in place of particularistic ones, and
3. expectations and duties in the role system become more specific.

It would be perhaps not less appropriate to say that Max Weber may be the first to have given the model of modernization by offering typology of rational and traditional. His social action ranges from traditional to rational and his authority ranges from traditional-personal to rational-legal-impersonal. Modern economic action is also a rational one for him. He equates rationalism with a societal characteristic of the European society.

Marion J. Levy and E.S.N. Eisenstadt, like Parsons, opined that the smooth modernization is possible only when initial structural and normative condition exists in developing countries.

Daniel Lerner is of the opinion that urbanization, modern education, development of communication system and economic development may be considered as main features of modernization. In his book *Modernization: Protest and Change,* E.S.N. Eisenstadt has expressed that modernization refers to changes in economic, political, cultural and social fields. Dipankar Gupta is very right to write that modernization means development of rationality and humanism in society.

Writing on the changes taking place in the Indian society and culture, M.N. Srinivas prefers the term 'Westernization' to 'modernization'. He defined his concept of Westernization as the changes brought about in the Indian society and culture as a result of over 150 years of British rule. Modernization, according to him, presupposes rationality of goals, which in the ultimate analysis could not be taken for granted, since human ends are based on value preferences and rationality could be predicted only of the means, not of the ends, of social action. Yogendra Singh finds problem with the term 'Westernization' because Srinivas equates it with the British impact on India, whereas, since independence, the impact of Russian and American versions of modernization in India has been considerable. This form of modernization has also not been free from the influence of implicit ideologies, for instance, the policy with regard to industrialization. In this field, the persistent controversy over the public versus private management and ownership of factories offers an ideological case in modernization. These value conflicts which today form an integral aspect of change and modernization in India cannot be adequately accounted for by a term like 'Westernization'. Moreover, for many new elite in India, as also in the new states of Asia, the term 'Westernization' has a pejorative connotation because of its association with former colonial domination of these countries by the West. It is, therefore, more value-loaded than the term 'modernization' which to us appears as a better substitute. Yogendra Singh wrote that modernization in India started mainly with the western contact through establishment of British rule. This contact had a special historicity, which brought about many far-reaching changes in culture and social structure of the Indian society. Cultural modernization started in forms of universalistic legal system, expansion of Western form of education, urbanization and industrialization, spread of new means of communication and transport and social reforms. Along with these modernizing norms, structural modernization also took place. For instance, rational bureaucratic systems of administration and judiciary, army and industrial bureaucracy, new class of business elite and entrepreneurs came into being.

There are two broad categories of approaches to modernization: structural and evolutionary. Preponderant in social sciences is rather the structural approach. The structural approach seeks to analyze modernization with the help of selected social or normative variables. For instance, Karl W. Deutsch used 'social mobilization' for political development, Daniel Lerner and Wilbu Schramm used 'growth of communication' and 'media exposure', David E. Apter and Lucian W. Pye used democratic political institutions and values, and M.J. Levy used 'technological and economic resources of society'. E.S.N. Eisenstadt says that for these modernization norms to take place a society must initially have cultural and structural autonomy.

The evolutionary approach takes modernization as a stage in the evolutionary process of change in the life of human society. There are two streams of evolutionary approach: dialectical (Marxist) and structural-functional. Structural-functional approach is based on organismic principle of change from simple to complex whereas dialectical approach finds in modernization an increasing class struggle at international level. Talcott Parsons' concept of 'evolutionary universals' relates to structural-functional analysis of evolutionary process of modernization.

The most significant characteristics of modern society are the predominance of rationalism, humanism, competitive democracy, market economy and welfare state. The modern society honours the dignity of each and every individual and guarantees welfare and freedom to everyone.

Domains of Modernization

Modernization takes place in all the three domains of society, viz., socio-cultural, political and economic, though the extent of modernization is not necessarily uniform in them.

Economic Modernization

Economic modernization refers to a change of outlook towards earning profit, rational economic activity, frequent use of sophisticated technology and consistent effort to bring about innovative changes in the production system. The agrarian economy, which was only consumption-oriented, has metamorphosed into the industrial one. The industrial economy has people with entrepreneurial temperament, profit motive with acquisitiveness and rational and scientific views towards economic enterprise and who make an excessive use of sophisticated modern technology. Even agriculture in the modern society has assumed an industrial character, in which the farmer is quite rational in farming. They use agricultural technology and try to produce according to the requirements of the market. The farming carried out by the farmer is quite scientific. In a pre-modern economy, agriculture was consumption-oriented and conventional methods were used to carry out farming.

The economic relations in modern economy are legal-contractual whereas in the traditional economy these relations were customary. Landlords had customary rights over tenant farmers and agricultural labourers and the wages paid by landlords to workers were only customarily decided.

Urbanization and economic modernization go together and promote each other. Urbanization spreads entrepreneurial and industrial culture. People under the influence of urban culture are oriented to rational economic action, have high achievement motivation, and are motivated to pursue profit-yielding enterprise. Urban culture promotes entrepreneurial personality. Urbanization is a process in which the workforce shifts from agriculture to manufacturing and other non-agrarian sectors. There is excessive use of technology in industrial and non-industrial sectors.

Increasing consumerism is yet another indicator of economic modernization. People are increasingly interested in excessive purchases. They develop the habit of consuming more and more and change the articles quite frequently. Globalization has played the role of a catalyst in the process of economic modernization.

Political Modernization

Modern political system was a great political change that followed the European Renaissance, which caused the separation of church from state. These two were united during the pre-Renaissance period. The revolutionary change that introduced the modern political systems founded on the principles of equality, liberty and democracy and the state was completely liberated from the control of the church and declared to be secular. Secular state means that the state will neither practise a religion nor interfere in the practice of religion by its citizens. It will also not allow any citizen to misuse religion in order to gain political mileage.

Democracy is the most acceptable and most modern form of government. There is hardly any state in the world which is not partly or wholly democratic. It is the most humanitarian political system. The basic preambles of democracy consist of equality, liberty and fraternity. People are politically conscious and alert to their rights and duties as citizens. A politically modern person takes active part in the political process of the country. The efforts are made to ensure that the elections in the country are free and fair and all the citizens have equal rights and opportunities to participate in the political processes. A healthy and successful political modernization is that in which we find a satisfied public.

A politically modern society is that in which civil society is quite vibrant and works as a watchdog in the interest of the countrymen. Civil society is activated when the state generally fails to shoulder its responsibilities and is unable to take care of its citizens. At this stage, non-governmental organizations (NGOs) play a significant role in undertaking the job of meeting the requirements of the people in a country. In India, about 1,600 NGOs are internationally recognized and work quite purposefully in the sectors like education, health and environmental protection.

Socio-cultural Modernization

Modernization is essentially a process of culture change, which brings about rational and scientific world view and new social values due to which changes in social, economic and political systems take place. Under the influence of modernization, the conspicuous changes that have taken place in the traditional Indian social structure and, for that matter, in most of traditional societies of the world are from authoritarianism to democracy, particularism to universalism, holism to individualism, ethnicity to humanism, dogmatism and emotionality to rationality, joint family to nuclear family, ascribed status to achieved status, inequality to equality, male chauvinism to women empowerment etc.

Indian society has undergone a good deal of modernization. The traditions and customs related to caste, family, marriage and religion have been influenced by modern values. The caste system, for example, has experienced drastic changes in its traditional characteristics. The occupational mobility, which was only minimal for many occupation-linked castes, has now become fast and diverse. No longer are people compelled to observe the traditional caste norms and style of living. No longer is the authority of a person exercised or acceptable merely for his being born in a higher caste. No longer exists the past obligatory, customary and exploitative rural *jajmani* economy. The process of sanskritization in which the lower castes, in order to enhance their position in society, not only tended to follow the culture and style of life of the higher castes but also refused to carry out the menial work they used to do for the higher castes during the medieval period of the 20th century was a result of modernization effect. From 1980s, the sanskritization process weakened as the lower castes took recourse under a greater impact of political modernization and started getting integrated to emerge as a formidable political force.

The differences in the characteristics of traditional and modern societies in these domains are as follows:

Traditional Society	*Modern Society*
Socio-cultural Characteristics	
Familialism	Individualism
Authoritarian structure of family	Democratic structure of family
Large size of family	Small size of family
Large kinship relations	Fewer kinship relations
Importance of ascribed status	Importance of achieved status
Predominantly primary relations	Predominantly secondary relations
Ascribed positions like caste	Achieved positions like class

cont'd...

cont'd...

Dogmatism	Rationalism and scientific outlook
Ethnicity	Plurality
Illiteracy	Literacy
Gender inequality	Gender neutrality
Fundamentalism	Liberalism
Political Characteristics	
Autocracy	Democracy
Fundamentalism	Secularism
Lack of individual freedom	Individual freedom
Imperial state	Welfare state
Customary laws	Written laws
Traditional personal authority	Rational impersonal authority
Nativeness	Citizenship
Personal army	Government army
Local body	Strong bureaucracy
Economic Characteristics	
Agrarian economy	Industrial economy
Customary economic relations	Contractual economic relations
Subsistence economy	Market economy
Conventional production and trade	Innovation and entrepreneurship
Hereditary occupation	Occupational mobility
Simple division of labour	Complex division of labour
Simple and crude technology	Modern technology

The above polarities are not neat and exclusivistic and have only heuristic significance. Different societies exist somewhere in between these polar opposite features depending on their access to technology, means of mass communication, other facilitating infrastructures and capacity to adapt to the new challenges of change. These positions of societies are not static but are constantly subjected to dynamism.

Changing Theoretical Perspectives of Modernization

Ever since 1960s, when the concept of modernization came to light, it has passed through many paradigm shifts in response to emerging challenges in the society. Every following decade till 1990s appears to have experienced a new conceptualization of modernization. Jeffrey Alexander (1994) in his essay "Modern, Anti, Post, and Neo: How social theories have tried to understand the 'New World' of our times" distinguishes four stages of theoretical construction in social sciences. In 1960s, the modernization theory constructed the western development as a universal model. Nation-building, participation, economic growth and cultural rationalization constituted the model for transformation of the less developed countries. The capitalist form of development became the ideal economic system.

In the 1970s came out the theory of underdevelopment, popularly known as dependency theory or the world system theory. This theory emerged out of the situation of exploitation of the resources of the less developed countries by the developed ones and thus keeping the former constantly dependent upon the latter. This view is radically opposed to the capitalist mode of development but it should not be treated as a Marxist view. Andre Gunder Frank and Immanuel Wallerstein have propounded the world system theories with only a minor difference in their approaches. Both agree that the capitalist development has built a world system but Wallerstein divides countries of the world into four regions: core, semi-periphery, periphery and external. Frank divides the countries into two categories, viz., metropolis and satellite.

These underdevelopment theories rejected the capitalist modernization theory and developed the optimism of mass controlled socialist-politico-economic system to replace it. But, the developments that took place in the late 1980s in the East Asian countries were sufficient to undermine the sustenance of the significance of world system theories. As a consequence, a 'post-modernist' approach to the understanding of the processes of development and modernization emerged. Thus, both modernization and underdevelopment theories were criticized by the post-modernists as outdated and used "great narratives" and multiple cultural and constructivist contingency theories.

Towards close of 1980s we saw the demise of USSR and the breakdown of communism and development and expansion of democracy and market economy in many Asian countries, including India. This stage is called by Jeffrey Alexander and Edward Tiryakian and Wolfgang Zapf as 'neo-modernism' or the 'modernization II' which promotes democracy and free economic development. Tiryakian has summarized the neo-modernization analysis as follows:

1. Modernization is the result of actions by individuals and collectives, not an automatic development of systems.
2. They seek new ways to achieve their goals and fulfil their values, but whether these aims can be accomplished will depend on their resources.
3. Modernization is not a consensual process, but a competition between modernizers, conservatives and bystanders.
4. Science is the major driving force, but religion and tradition must not be underestimated.
5. The general criterion for the success of modernization is the welfare development of the whole population.
6. Centres of modernization may change and move.
7. Modernization is not continuous-linear; it also has cycles and regressive crises.

Modernization in India

Modernization in India has not been all-pervasive. This process did not lead to any serious breakdown in the Indian society. Eisenstadt says that Indian society did not face any breakdown because of its peculiar structural conditions, particularly the independence of cultural system from the political system. Both, the system of polity and the system of caste stratification, have always remained independent in India. Modernization mainly developed as a sub-structure and sub-culture without pervasive expansion in all sectors of life. Yogendra Singh is of the view that there would be no possibility of major structural breakdown, even during the second phase of modernization in the Indian society. Legislations and the processes, such as urbanization, industrialization, proliferation of education and politicization have brought about many positive changes, including abolition of social inequalities and untouchability. In India, modernization has not replaced tradition; instead, the traditional structures and loyalties are being mobilized for objectives which are essentially modern. Caste and religious loyalties and folk songs and dances are being increasingly used in democratic political processes in the country. Certain traditions have been reinforced, religious practices and rituals are being modernized by using modern technology and mass media. However, modernization in India has not been consistent. In some aspects of the micro-structures, such as caste and family, there has been modernization, whereas some others are uninfluenced by modern values.

Changes in the Caste System

The old rigid caste structure with neat hierarchy and segregative norms has undergone drastic change. It has adapted to the modern institutions. Now, cases of inter-caste marriages are not unknown, untouchability, as it was, is almost disappeared and affirmative action has enhanced the social status of many lower caste people and families, if not of the whole caste. However, caste still persists in many ways. Some political parties have been found, for historical reasons, associated with particular castes. The election process in the country is indeed democratic but the use of power and caste loyalties by some people to some extent may not be ruled out. The recent debate on the reservation issue has to some extent vulgarized the existence of caste.

Caste has two features – cultural and structural. The cultural characteristics of caste have definitely undergone drastic change, adapting to modern values, as a result of urbanization, industrialization, spread of education and state intervention, but the structural aspect of caste system continues to sustain many of its features essentially due to the fact that despite all active efforts and policy formulations, the Indian government has not been able to implement agrarian reforms and reduce agrarian inequalities in villages. The major factor responsible for social distance among different castes in villages, as is visible even today, is the traditionally continued land-based inequality and still prevailing factual illiteracy. The statistics of literacy, as given by the state, do not present the real picture. The enrolment and dropping out of the scheduled caste, OBC and women students at the very primary education level is indeed pathetic and must be countered.

More significant to analyze is the interactional aspect of caste system in the country. The segregation among different castes that existed in traditional Indian society is observed as continuing even today in many ways with the only difference that earlier it was culturological and less taken as alienating whereas, today, due to political modernization and identity consciousness leading to the formation of caste associations and integrations, it has sharpened on political lines leading occasionally to eruption of caste rivalry or even caste war. The power structure has drastically changed eroding the power of the higher, particularly the landed castes. The *jajmani* system has been completely rejected by the traditional occupational castes and no longer exists the practice of compulsory inheritance of family occupations. The movement against serving the other castes (landlords) by traditional occupation started immediately after independence, which resulted in the abolition of the zamindari system.

The emergence of caste associations and caste politics exhibits the process of modernization but some traditional norms continue. Lloyd Rudolph characterizes caste association as having the mixed attributes both of the ascriptive and voluntary groups leading to what he calls 'shadow society' which has a modernizing impact without overtly replacing the traditional institution of caste. Yogendra Singh writes that modernity has entered into Indian character and society but it has done so through assimilation, not replacement.

Changes in the Family System

In India, the old traditional joint family system no longer continues. It was patriarchal in nature, its size was large, status of women in the family was very low, members of family had no individual identity, and the decision-making power lied exclusively with the eldest male member of the family. The members were the blood relations, and had property, residence and hearth, and even worship, in common. The members in a joint family could be of three or more generations, and were morally bound to one another by rights and duties.

Indian family system has undergone drastic change in response to development in terms of industrialization, education and urbanization. Industrialization and urbanization, leading to accelerated rate of rural-urban migration, diversification of gainful economic activities and individual-friendly property laws, have had consequential impact in terms of drastic reduction in the size of family in the country. Most families, particularly in urban areas, have only one or two generation members (i.e., parents and their unmarried children). But, it does not mean that the Indian family is becoming nuclear. Actually, the existence of nuclear family in India is only circumstantial.

The culture and attitude of people is still in favour of the joint family system. Existing nuclear families in the country (whatsoever is the number) are only a temporary phase. In reality, the joint family has been a tradition of India. The nuclear families also existed though it is not an Indian tradition.

The family in the country is no longer patriarchal in true sense of the term; it exists as a patri-local household. There is a lot of individual autonomy and no longer is decision-making the exclusive right of the eldest male member of the family. The family is now essentially democratic and most of the decisions in the family are taken collectively. However, the extent of autonomy and democracy may vary from region to region, community to community and caste to caste, depending upon the degree of its adaptation of the modern values and the urban way of life.

The family in India is passing through a contradiction. Even educated males, though are in favour of modern education for their girl children, continue to expect them to remain inside homes and have their decisions be taken by the elder male members, particularly their parents. They also wish them to be working women but continue to expect them to work in the house and, in some cases, observe purdah. As most people have now started taking up jobs in different parts of the country leaving their parental family behind, they are having separate households. Such small households look forward to maintaining relationship with the parental family and extending help and support to it. Yogendra Singh writes on modernization, as taking place in the Indian family system, in this way:

> Changes in the structure and function of joint families in India are thus following a reconciliatory pattern, a pattern common in the structural changes in the Indian society. In mate selection, the principle of personal choice, especially in urban families, is today increasingly reconciled with parents' approval; the wife's freedom in middle-class homes to work outside in offices and schools operates within the traditional

framework of the husband's approval and sometimes the approval of husband's or even wife's parents. Such reconciliations are, however, not without tension which is an inalienable aspect of social change. Despite these changes, traditional views on joint family still prevail.

Passing away of the traditional joint family system and not being replaced by nuclear family system has resulted into a new kind of family set-up in the country. Today, most families form as nuclear kind of households and continue to exist as constituents of joint families. Therefore, today, it has become more relevant to study households rather than joint or nuclear families.

Macro-structural Changes and Modernization

Industrialization, urbanization and democratization are the processes of macro-structural changes. The changes in these fields have exhibited modernization effect but resilience to the traditional structural realities continues to be effective showing again a process of assimilation, instead of replacement.

The history of modern industrial development in India is not old. It started hardly one and a half century ago but gathered acceleration only half a century before. There has indeed been impressive industrial growth over the last few decades but a minute analysis would be required to find out the sociological reality of industrial modernization in the country. The ideology of industrial modernization of India represented a combination of capitalist and socialist approaches of development, which led to the policy of mixed economy and lasted until the New Economic Policy (NEP) was adopted by the government in 1991 in favour of liberalization, privatization and globalization.

Entrepreneurial development is a key to industrial expansion. It is also an indication of industrial modernization. Entrepreneurs are the real contributors to structural modernization in society. But, though, there is quite a good deal of modernization in the business sector, the traditional social structure has inhibited a great deal – the acceleration of entrepreneurial supply in the country. Not that only entrepreneurial supply has been sluggish and motivation for self-employment has not caught up, the social spaces have also not been uniformly conducive for the emergence of entrepreneurship in the country. It is only after 1990 due to the NEP that the entrepreneurial supply and industrial performance at global standards gained impetus.

Changes in the Education System

Education is an effort of the senior people to transfer their knowledge to the younger members of society. It is thus an institution, which plays a vital role in integrating an individual with his society and in maintaining the perpetuation of culture. Emile Durkheim defines education as "the influence exercised by the adult generation upon those who are not yet ready for adult life". He further maintains that "society can survive only if there exists among its members a sufficient degree of homogeneity. The homogeneity is perpetuated and reinforced by education. A child through education learns basic rules, regulations, norms and values of society".

Education thus is an essential prerequisite of modernization. It enables people to know the world beyond their own surroundings and transforms them to become rationalist and humanist in outlook and world view. However, it has to be kept in mind that the education has got modernized and in turn is contributing to the process of modernization of the Indian society.

The traditional education system of India was quite different from the contemporary one. In traditional Indian society, the number of educational institutions was too small and the content of education was esoteric and essentially related with religion, philosophy, metaphysics and scriptural subjects.

The education was confined to the 'twice-born' castes and the upper classes. The organizational structure was ascriptive and hereditary. The lower castes, particularly the scheduled castes, were denied education. Even today, the Madrassah education among Muslims is largely based on religion, philosophy and scriptural messages. Shishu Mandirs also have religion and tradition as parts of curriculum.

Modern education is exoteric, open and liberal. The world-view is scientific-rational, the theme consists of freedom, equality, humanism and denial of faith in dogma and superstitions. The course contents are rationalistic and in tune with the needs of the present-day society. Science and technology, grammar and literature, social philosophy, history and culture, geography and ecology, agriculture and horticulture comprise the vast range of subjects which are taught in schools, colleges and universities. The modern education lays emphasis on the subjects like freedom, nationality, law, human rights, democracy and scientific world view. The other parts of education are the co-curricular and extra-curricular activities, which are often organized for total personality development of a student.

The modern education is change-oriented and, therefore, courses are modified time and again corresponding to the changes taking place in society at large so as to keep pace with the needs of the changing situations in the wake of fast-changing industrial society.

The present industrial society has opened up a multiplicity of occupations and professions and each one of them is associated with scientific knowledge and skills. It is a society of complex division of labour and requires people with specialized knowledge. The modern education fulfils needs of the industrial economy. A vast range of subjects like medicine, health, engineering, management and law have become hot areas of professionalization and specialization today.

Problems of Educational Modernization

There are two serious problems of education in India, which still continue even after 63 years of independence: one, still education is not freely and easily available to all in the country; two, the education system is still not fully modernized in the country.

Unequal Educational Opportunity

There is no uniform and equal opportunity of education in the country. Education in the country is elitist in the sense that there are two educational systems in country and both of them are distinct from each other in terms of their standard and recognition. On one hand are the government schools suffering from complete negligence on the part of management and teachers. Teachers seldom go to school and if they do go they do it without any seriousness.

Despite constitutional provisions of equal opportunity for education to all in the country and declaration of as a fundamental right, all children do not go to school at initiation level and those who are enrolled, by the time they reach intermediate level, about 90 per cent drop out. A large population among weaker sections in the country is found away from the pursuit of education.

On the other hand, there are private schools meant for different social classes ranging from the lower-middle class to the upper class of society. These private schools are so expensive that quite a large number of children are prohibited from the education. The existing class differentiation in society is further reinforced by this distinct education.

According to the 2001 Census, 65.38 per cent population of the country is literate, out of which 75.96 per cent were males and 54.28 per cent were females. Over the period of a decade between 1991 and 2001, the growth in literacy has been 13.75 per cent.

Educational Organizations and Course Contents

Our education system is no longer traditional. It is quite modern – structurally and functionally. No one is denied the opportunity of education and anyone can teach, if qualified. The content of education is also modern. Liberty, humanism, freedom, morality and democracy, science and technology are the core subjects taught in schools.

However, we cannot boast of having a fully modern education system in the country. For example, the Madrassah education among Muslims is not a modern one though they claim to include the core contents of modern education. But, their emphasis on religious education leaves schools miles away from modernity. Rashtriya Swayamsevak Sangh (RSS) run schools too may not be accepted as fully modern since they have religious overtones in the schooling pattern.

Indian government has sanctioned minority status to the schools run by Muslim and Christian communities. These institutions are not allowed to run as purely modern educational institutions. Thus sectarianism and cultural relativism are reinforced by such educational institutions.

Quite often debates take place on the legitimacy of the Madrassah education in India. Some even question their national allegiance and some others blame them for breeding fundamentalist personalities threatening communal harmony. No substantial evidence has been available so far to confirm any of the doubts, but one cannot approve of such educational patterns in the era of globalized world system as is emerging where an absolutely secular attitude, widely accepted language for communication, skillfulness and advanced technology to control modern economy in world market are required.

Similarly, Saraswati Vidya Mandir schools, run by the RSS a Hindu organization, did adopt modern contents of education but one may not deny that the environment of schools is charged with the existence of an overtone of Hindu traditions derived from mythologies and religious scriptures.

Political Modernization in India

Before the 17th century, in the pre-industrial political system of Europe, the state and the church were combined together. Kingdoms ruled and religion controlled the governing system. It is with Renaissance and Industrial Revolution that the state was disjointed from the church and there emerged the idea of sovereign nation-state. The political ideology on which the states were grounded was the democracy. The state consisted of citizens, who not only enjoyed liberty and equality, but also freedom of speech and expression of views, and of taking up any economic activity and participation in political processes frankly. India is one of the modernized political systems of the world. Democracy is the most modernized system. Secularism is the ideology of a democracy. With the attainment of independence in 1947, India adopted political democracy. At that time, two mutually antagonistic politico-economic systems existed: capitalism of the Western Europe and communism of the Eastern Europe. India opted for a democratic political system and ever since independence has been cherishing the goal of democracy with a federal set-up based on well-formulated and sanctum sanctorum constitution. Our constitution guarantees to every citizen liberty and equality and also is committed to social justice for those who have been socially, politically and economically deprived for centuries.

India is perhaps the biggest and one of the most successful parliamentary democracies in the world. It is a well-established and mature, sovereign and democratic nation-state, guaranteeing full citizenship to its people. The country is well-founded on the principles of equality, liberty, human rights and individual's dignity, social justice and separation of religion from politics. People enjoy freedom of speech, participate in movements and agitations, and form or participate in political parties. This is all testimony to successful continuance of political democracy in the country. Except a single episode of the imposition of emergency in the country in 1975 by the then Prime Minister Indira Gandhi, which was outrightly rejected by people of the country routing out her political party – the Congress – in the next election. Since then, no party could wield dominating and dynastic rule in the country. This trend is reflective of growing political consciousness among people of the country.

It is significant to note that over the last two and a half decades, there has been a tremendous arousal of political awakening among the socio-cultural communities of the country, which were earlier denied a dignified social position and political participation. But, the spread of education and other processes, like transportation, communication and urbanization, have contributed significantly to political awareness among the deprived sections of Indian society, which have grown now into significant and formidable political force in the country. Dalit movement has acquired a decisive position to determine the political trend of the country. Other Backward Classes (OBCs) are the other significant social groups that have evolved into a significant political force. Political parties, such as Bahujan Samaj Party (BSP) and Samajwadi Party (SP), are identified with the dalits and OBCs of the country. Though these parties are considered to have only a regional status but they indeed have crucial role to play in national politics. A small combination and permutation changes the political face of the country. Ascendance of BSP to Uttar Pradesh's rule with absolute majority in the recent elections and SP's ouster from power would be an appropriate example of this kind of development.

Lapses in Political Modernization

There is, however, not so much to be pessimistic about the hiccups in the democratic political processes in the country. This is so particularly if we keep in mind that most countries, despite becoming independent more or less at the time when India did, have not been able to establish a modern democratic political system as India has been able to do. They have non-democratic political system – be it dictatorship, military rule or kingship.

However, it is not all to be cheerful about the political modernization in the country. The following are the points on which we may consider that Indian democracy is confronting some challenges to which it has to respond sincerely, firmly and intelligently in order to boast of being a successful democracy:

1. Traditional power structure continues to influence, to some extent, the political process in the country. The caste-based privileged class dominates the process.
2. The country may not boast of having free, fearless and fair elections. Violence and obstructions in election processes are not uncommon. Certain sections of society are denied participation in political processes of the country.
3. The Indian caste system has been a socially and culturally segmentary hierarchical structure. This purely undemocratic social system has changed most of its traditional characteristics. It has, in particular, renounced its segmentary traits but now has unfortunately grown into a tool being used to influence political processes of the country. Though undeclared, but a few political parties are considered to have strong caste base and identities.
4. There are parties and groups which have their religious identities. Their presence and political activism has posed a great challenge to the secular character of Indian democracy.
5. From the point of view of elections, as and when due, freedom of speech, choosing the occupation, protective discrimination and social justice etc., we can confirm that the Indian democracy has succeeded. But if we consider the scenario in terms of governance and the welfare programmes of governments, we find absolute failures. For

example, there is rampant corruption, law and order is questionable, people's social and economic security is not sufficiently secured, farmers commit suicide largely due to the inability of repayment of loans etc. As far as election processes are concerned, we cannot boast of having absolutely free elections. A good number of people in villages are not allowed by the wealthy and otherwise influential people to cast their vote if they are not in their favour. The last two elections in Uttar Pradesh and Bihar are, however, the testimony to a sincere and active interest taken by the Election Commission of India that, in due course of time, elections in the country would be genuinely free, fair and fearless.

6. For the last two decades, there has been serious criminalization of Indian polity. Most of the criminals have either joined hands with politicians or have turned politicians themselves changing the face of Indian politics. People have shaky faith in the government and their representatives. Civil society is consequently becoming stronger to safeguard the interest of the masses.

Bibliography

Amin, Samir. 1976. *Unequal Development: An Essay on the Social Formulation of Peripheral Capitalism.* Hassocks: Harvester.

Baran, Paul. 1973. *The Political Economy of Growth.* Harmondsworth: Penguin.

Benedix, Richard. 1960. *Max Weber: An Intellectual Portrait*. Garden City, NY: Doubleday.

Berna, James J. 1960. *Industrial Entrepreneurship in Madras State.* London: Asia Publishing House.

Brozen, Yale. 1954. "Determinants of Entrepreneurial Ability", *Social Research*, Vol. 21, p. 238.

Chaudhary, Asim. 1975. *Private Economic Power in India: A Study in Genesis and Concentration.* New Delhi: Peoples Publishing House.

Cocharan, T.C. 1960. "Cultural Factors in Economic Growth", *Journal of Economic History*, Vol. XX (December).

——. 1962. *Entrepreneurship in the Argentine Culture.* Philadelphia: University of Pennsylvania Press.

Datta, Amalan. 1957. *Essays on Economic Development*. Calcutta: Bookland Pvt. Ltd.

Desai, A.R. 1961. *Rural Sociology in India*. Bombay: Popular Prakshan.

DiMaggio, P. 1990. "Cultural Aspects of Economic Organization and Behaviour" in R. Friedland and A.F. Robertson (eds.), *Beyond the Market Place: Rethinking Economy and Society*. New York: Aldine.

Dube, S.C. 1958. *India's Changing Villages*. Ithaca, New York: Cornell University Press.

Evans, G.H.. 1949. "The Entrepreneur and Economic Theory", *American Economic Review*.

Fischer, Claude S. 2005. "Theories of Urbanism" in J. Lin and C. Mele (eds.), *The Urban Sociology*. New York: Routledge.

Frederickson, George M. 1981. *White Supremacy*, Oxford University Press.

Fukuyama, Francis. 1992. *End of History and the Last Man*. New York: The Free Press.

——. 1989. *Our Post Human Future: Consequences of Biotechnology Revolution*. New York: The Free Press.

Giddens, Anthony. 2001. *Sociology*, IV edition. UK: Polity Press.

Gens, Herbert. 2005. "Urbanism and Suburbanism: A Reevaluation of Definitions" in J. Lin and C. Mele (eds.), *The Urban Sociology*. New York: Routledge.

Hagen, E.E. 1962. *On the Theory of Social Change: How Economic Growth Begins?* London: Tavistock.

——. 1971. The "Transition in Columbia" in Peter Kilby, *Entrepreneurship and Economic Development*. New York: The Free Press.

Harrison, David. 1888. *Sociology of Modernization and Development*. New York: Routledge.

Holmstrom, Mark. 2007. *South Indian Factory Workers*. Cambridge: Cambridge University Press.

Hoselitz, B.F. 1964. "A Sociological Approach to Economic Development" in D. Novak and R. Lekachman (eds.), *Development of Sociology*. New York.

Huntington, Samuel P. 1968. *Political Order in Changing Societies*. London: Yale University Press.

——. 1976. "The Change to Change", in Cyril E. Black (ed.) *Comparative Modernization*, New York: The Free Press.

Iyer, Lalitha. 1991. *Women Entrepreneurs: Challenges and Strategies*. New Delhi: Friedrich Stiftung (FES).

Kapp, K.W. 1963. *Hindu Culture, Economic Development and Economic Planning in India*. Bombay: Asia Publishing House.

Kilby, Peter (ed.). 1971. *Entrepreneurship and Economic Development*. New York: The Free Press.

Kunz, Virginia Brainard. 1966. *The Germans in America*. Minneapolis: Lerner Publications Co.

Masihi, Edwin. 2004. "Voluntary Organizations and Social Change" in S.N. Pawar, J.B. Ambekar and D. Srikant (eds.) *NGOs and Development: The Indian Scenario*. Jaipur: Rawat Publications.

McClelland, D. 1961. *The Achieving Society*. New York: The Free Press.

Morris, D. 1967. "Values as an Obstacle to Economic Growth in South Asia: A Historical Survey", *Journal of Economic History*, Vol. 27.

Myrdal, Gunnar. 1970. *Challenge of World Poverty*. Allen Lane: The Penguin Press.

North, Douglass C. 1990. *Institutions, Institutional Change and Institutional Performance*. Cambridge: Cambridge University Press.

OECD. 1997. *Globalization and Small and Medium Enterprises (SMEs)*. Vol. I.

Ostergaard, L. 1994. *Gender and Development*. London: Routledge.

Pandit, D.P. 1957. "Creative Response in Indian Economy", *Economic and Political Weekly*, February 23 and March 2.

Parsons, T. 1964. "Evolutionary Universals in Society", *American Sociological Review*, 29,(3) Jun.

Pawar, S.N. et al. (eds.). 2004. *NGOs and Development*. Jaipur: Rawat Publications.

Piore, Michael. 1996. "Review of the Handbook of Economic Sociology". *Journal of Economic Literature*, 34, pp. 741–754

Planning Commission, 2001. "Report of the Study Group on Development of Small Scale Enterprises". Government of India: New Delhi.

Polanyi, Karl. 1944. *The Great Transformation.* New York: Rinehart.

Prabhu, P.H. 1940. *Hindu Social Organization.* Bombay: Popular Prakashan.

Ramaswami, Uma. 1983. *Work, Union and Community.* New Delhi: Oxford University Press.

Redlitch, Fritz. 1955. "Entrepreneurship in Initial Stages of Industrialization with Special Reference of Germany", *Weltwirschaftliches Archiv*, Vol. 75.

——. 1958 "Business Leadership: Diverse Origins and Diverse Forms", *Economic Development and Cultural Change,* Vol. VI. No. 3.

Rippy, J.F. 1931. *The Capitalists and the Columbia.* New York: Vanguard.

Rudolph, L.I. and Rudolph, S.H. 1987. *In Pursuit of Laxmi.* University of Chicago Press.

Samuelson, Kurt. 1961. *Religion and Economic Action,* Geoffrey French (Trans.) (Stockholm).

Sarngadharan, M. and Beegam, S.R. 1995. *Women Entrepreneurship: Institutional Support and Problems,* New Delhi: Discovery Publications.

Schumpeter, J.A. 1967. *The Theory of Economic Development.* New York: Oxford University Press.

Seth, N.R. 2004. "The Field of Labour", *Sociological Bulletin,* Vol. 53.

Sengupta, Nirmal. 2003. "The New Institutional Economics: Its Perimeters and Promises". Paper presented in the 86th conference of Indian Economic Association.

Sharma, K.L. and Gupta, Dipankar. 1991. *Country-Town Nexus.* Jaipur: Rawat Publications.

Sharma, K.L. 1975. *Entrepreneurial Performance in Role Perspective.* New Delhi: Abhinav Publications.

Siddharthan, N.S. and Lal, K. 2003. "Liberalization and Growth of Firms in India", *Economic and Political Weekly,* May 17.

Singh, Sheobahal, 1985. "Relevance of Social Factors in Entrepreneurial Growth", *Journal of Sociological Studies,* Vol. 4, January.

——. 1985. *Entrepreneurship and Social Change.* Jaipur: Rawat Publications.

——. 2001. "Gender and Entrepreneurship". Project report submitted to the ICSSR, New Delhi.

Singh, Kamla. 1992. *Women Entrepreneurs.* New Delhi: Ashish Publishing House.

Singh, Yogendra. 1973. *Modernization of Indian Tradition.* Delhi: Thompson Press.

——. 1993. *Social Change in India: Crisis and Resilience.* New Delhi: Har-Anand Publications.

Sovani, N.V. 1966. *Urbanization and Urban India.* New York: Asia Publishing House.

Sowell, Thomas. 1983. *Economics and Politics of Race.* New York: William Morrow and Company, INC.

Subrahmanya, M.H. Bala. 2003. "Technological Innovations in Small Enterprises: Comparative Study of Bangalore and North-East England", *Economic and Political Weekly,* May 24.

Sujata, K. 1982. "Dynamics of Family Firms in India: An Exploratory Analysis of the Role of Family and Kinship in Industrial Entrepreneurship". M.Phil. Dissertation, Jawahar Lal Nehru University, New Delhi.

Swedberg, Richard. 1998. *Max Weber and the Idea of Economic Sociology.* Princeton NJ: Princeton University Press.

Todaro, Michael R. 1977. *Economic Development of the Third World.* New York: The Free Press.

Toffler, Alvin. 1970. *Future Shock.* New York: Random House.

Tripathi, D. 1970. "Indian Entrepreneurship in Historical Perspective: A Reinterpretation", *Economic and Political Weekly,* Vol. VI. No. 22.

——. 1997. *Historical Roots of Industrial Entrepreneurship in India and Japan.* New Delhi: Manohar Publishers.

Vinzey, M.D. 1987. *Women Entrepreneurship in India.* Delhi: Mittal Pub.

Virmani, Arvind. 2002. "A New Development Paradigm: Employment, Entitlement and Empowerment", *Economic and Political Weekly,* No. 22.

Weber, Max. 1947. *The Theory of Social and Economic Organization.* New York: The Free Press.

——. 1958. *Religion of India: The Sociology of Hinduism*. Glencoe, Illinois.

Williamson, Oliver E. 1985. *The Economic Institutions of Capitalism.* New York: The Free Press

——. 2000. "The New Institutional Economics, Taking Stock, Looking Ahead", *Journal of Economic Literature.*

Wirth, Louis. 2005. "Urbanism as a Way of Life" in J. Lin and C. Mele (eds.), *The Urban Sociology*. New York: Routledge.

Wisskopt, T.E. "China and India: A Comparative Survey of Performance in Economic Development", *Economic and Political Weekly*, February. Annual Number.

Young, F.W. 1971. "A Macro-sociological Interpretation of Entrepreneurship" in Peter Kilby (ed.), *Entrepreneurship and Economic Development*. New York: The Free Press.

Index